PIONEER PAPER NO. 3

Work and Welfare in Massachusetts

An Evaluation of the ET Program

June O'Neill

Published by

PIONEER INSTITUTE FOR PUBLIC POLICY RESEARCH
Boston, Massachusetts
1990

Pioneer Institute is an independent, non-profit research organization funded by individuals, corporations, and foundations. Pioneer Papers and Dialogues are published for educational purposes, to assist policymakers and to broaden public understanding of critical social and economic issues. Views expressed in the Institute's publications are those of the authors and not necessarily those of the Pioneer staff, advisors, or directors nor should they be construed as an attempt to influence any election or legislative action.

Library of Congress Cataloging-in-Publication Data

O'Neill, June.
    Work and welfare in Massachusetts : an evaluation of the
ET program / June O'Neill
    (Pioneer paper ; no. 3)
    Includes bibliographical references.
    ISBN 0-929930-03-7 : $10.00
    1. Welfare recipients — Employment — Massachusetts. 2. Aid to
families with dependent children programs — Massachusetts.
  I. Title. II. Series.
HV98.M39054   1990
362.5'84'09744 — dc20   90-34066

Pioneer Institute
for Public Policy Research

Pioneer Institute is a public policy research organization that specializes in the support, distribution and promotion of scholarly research on Massachusetts public policy issues. Its main program — the Pioneer Paper series — consists of research projects commissioned from area scholars. The Institute publishes these papers and communicates the research results to decision-makers in government and opinion leaders in business, academia, and the media. Pioneer Institute qualifies under IRS rules for 501 (c)(3) tax-exempt status.

Acknowledgements

This study reflects the dedicated work of many people to whom the author is grateful. Walter McManus, a former member of the Center for the Study of Business and Government, worked on initial stages of the study. Excellent research assistance and computer programming was provided by Matthew Cohen, Alexander Fudukidis, Hengzhong Liu and T. Jithendranathan. Eva Mattina and other staff at the Center worked diligently to lend secretarial support and other assistance throughout.

While the policy analysts who offered comments on early drafts of this study are in no way responsible for the author's conclusions, their suggestions, reflections, and in several cases, detailed comments were borne in mind by Professor O'Neill in the preparation of the final study. Pioneer Institute and Professor O'Neill gratefully acknowledge the helpful advice of the following experts:

Burt Barnow, Health and Sciences International
Linda Datcher-Loury, Tufts University
Richard Freeman, Harvard University
Steve Garasky, U.S. Department of Health and Human Services
Nathan Glazer, Harvard University
David Long, Manpower Demonstration Research Corporation
Charles Murray, Manhattan Institute
Richard P. Nathan, State University of New York
Kate W. O'Beirne, Heritage Foundation
Attiat Ott, Clark University
Alice Rivlin, Brookings Institution
Michael Wiseman, University of Wisconsin

Desktop Publishing:
    Kathryn Ciffolillo

Printing:
    Davis Press
    Worcester, Massachusetts

Table of Contents

List of Tables and Figures

Appendix Tables

Pioneer Institute recognizes the generous support of its members. It is only with your support — financial and otherwise — that Pioneer can continue to publish studies and sponsor educational forums and discussions.

Thank you.

Foreword

Most Massachusetts citizens applaud the concept of improving the job skills of those on welfare as a means of enabling its recipients to become self-sufficient. In 1983, Massachusetts began the Employment and Training Choices program, otherwise known as ET, to do just that. Since then, it has become one of the Commonwealth's most talked about social policy projects, yet has remained largely unexamined by independent scholars. In an attempt to contribute an in-depth and constructive critique of the program's performance, Pioneer commissioned this monograph in 1988 with June O'Neill, a professor of economics at Baruch College and a leading public policy analyst.

This book is the culmination of almost two years of hard work by a large number of dedicated people. Indeed, the long list of those who provided their comments and advice to us and to Professor O'Neill includes many leading public policy scholars and researchers. While there was not always complete agreement on every issue — the group represented a wide range of political and philosophical points of view — everyone who participated in our "peer review" process was impressed with the quality and depth of the work.

Professor O'Neill's fundamental conclusion about ET is clear: the program has not been as successful as proponents suggest. Her careful analysis shows that instead of saving the taxpayers money as advocates claim, ET has been costly and has contributed little or nothing to a reduction in the welfare caseload in Massachusetts. She suggests policy changes to make the program more cost-effective. Specifically, she recommends that the Commonwealth shift the program's focus away from maximizing numbers of job placements at priority wages and toward assisting inexperienced workers and others who are difficult to place. To accomplish this, she suggests modifying the reward structure for ET contractors and eliminating the wage floor for priority jobs. She also recommends that participation in ET be made obligatory. Her final suggestion is that the Commonwealth reconsider its current emphasis on high-cost formal day care. Instead, more flexible and lower cost child care arrangements could be made available to a larger number of working mothers.

We hope that people who see the need for "restructuring" state programs and are serious about devising concrete strategies to improve ET and programs like it, will benefit from Professor O'Neill's analysis and critique.

Pioneer is founded on the premise that scholarly analysis is an essential prerequisite to achieving sensible solutions to social and economic problems in the Commonwealth. We are pleased to offer this monograph as a contribution to the local and national discussion concerning welfare reform and job placement and training programs.

LOVETT C. PETERS
Chairman, Board of Directors

Boston, Massachusetts
April, 1990

1

Introduction and Overview

Ever since the welfare explosion of the late 1960s legislators and administrators have attempted to devise programs that would encourage welfare recipients to "work their way off welfare" and thereby become self-sufficient. One of the most ambitious and widely publicized programs of recent years has been the Employment and Training Choices program, known as ET, which was introduced by Governor Michael Dukakis in Massachusetts in October of 1983. According to Governor Dukakis,

> The ET program grew out of an awareness that welfare, while necessary and important in providing temporary help for families in need, can become a spiraling trap which decreases its victims' self-respect and sense of responsibility and increases their dependence.... It (ET) provides welfare recipients with a route out of poverty by helping them overcome whatever their own barriers to self-sufficiency might be. Barriers include illiteracy, an inability to speak English, insufficient education, a lack of marketable skills or work experience, the high cost and inadequate supply of child care, or the prospect of losing Medicaid (Dukakis and Kanter 1988).

Massachusetts has devoted considerable resources to the ET program — $240 million in state funds and $84 million in federal funds over a six-year period. A wide variety of employment services are offered to welfare recipients including assistance in career planning and job search, and training in basic education and job skills. Although Massachusetts is one of many states offering such services, it is unique in the size of the effort and the generosity of support services offered. For example, Massachusetts finances high-cost child care services for AFDC recipients while participating in ET and for at least one year after taking a job, and provides particularly intensive educational training programs. As a result, expenditures per participant in ET were approximately $2,000 in 1988, considerably higher than in other states offering employment and training programs. In a comparison with three other states offering programs, the General Accounting Office (GAO) found that Massachusetts spent the most — three times as much per participant as Michigan and seven times as much as Texas (GAO 1988).

No one questions the goals and objectives of the ET program. Most people would rather have welfare recipients working instead of collecting welfare, and most people would agree that many of the adults on AFDC are less educated and less qualified for better jobs than the population overall and might therefore benefit from training. Thus the relatively high expenditures on ET can prove worthwhile if the extra dollars spent produce additional gains.

According to the Massachusetts Department of Public Welfare, ET saved the taxpayers $280 million (net of costs) by placing 67,000 welfare recipients into jobs over the six-year period — October, 1983 to September, 1989. This estimate implies that the AFDC caseload in Massachusetts would have been at least 50 percent higher in 1989 — an incredibly large effect.

Claims such as these have been made repeatedly by the Dukakis administration and have been widely circulated in the media as evidence of the program's success. In fact, the favorable publicity for ET is believed to have contributed to the passage of the Family Support Act of 1988.[1] However, the Massachusetts Department of Public Welfare has not yet published any analysis backing up their claims.

The central task of this study is to measure the extent to which the ET program has reduced the welfare caseload and saved taxpayers money. In order to measure the true impact of ET on the caseload one must have a technique for distinguishing between changes in the caseload induced by the program and changes that would have occurred even in the absence of the program. This is important because as several recent studies have shown, the welfare caseload is not static. A substantial proportion of welfare recipients leave the caseload quickly — a majority by the end of two years. According to the Massachusetts DPW, prior to ET (fiscal year 1983) case closings in Massachusetts averaged close to 4,000 per month, and half of these closings were due to recipients taking jobs.

In view of these considerations, the Massachusetts DPW is likely to have overstated the success of ET because their estimates are based on the unlikely premise that none of the 67,000 ET participants placed in jobs over a six-year period would have found jobs on their own. Yet everything that we know about the dynamics of caseload turnover nationwide and in Massachusetts suggests that many of those placed by ET would have found jobs in the absence of the ET program.

In this study, we have constructed two statistical frameworks to help answer the question of what would have happened to the welfare caseload in the absence of the ET program. In addition, we have

---

[1]   This federal law, among other things, amends the AFDC program by creating new work-related programs for AFDC recipients and establishing a new program of child care assistance and extended Medicaid coverage for families leaving AFDC. Many of these provisions resemble the design of the ET program.

weighed this information against data on program costs to determine the net savings generated by the program. Finally, we have recommended steps that Massachusetts officials might consider taking to improve the cost-effectiveness of the ET program.

Concerning the caseload, we find that ET has not led to any significant reduction in the welfare rolls in Massachusetts. Moreover, work participation among single mothers in Massachusetts — the target population of ET — has not been increased by the program.

These findings are based on two types of statistical analysis employing different data and methodologies. The first analysis examines changes in the welfare caseload in Massachusetts from 1970 to the end of 1987. It estimates the effect of the ET program on the caseload after controlling for important economic and demographic factors and policy changes that would be expected to influence welfare participation. The AFDC-Basic caseload (essentially, female-headed families with children) and the unemployed parent (UP) caseload were examined separately, because of likely differences in the response of single mothers and unemployed fathers to external events and to ET. The Basic caseload has typically accounted for 95 percent or more of the total caseload.

The results suggest that little if any of the decline in either the Basic or UP programs during the 1980s can reasonably be attributed to the ET program. Changes in the economy and in the AFDC benefit level and especially the effects of the Omnibus Budget Reconciliation Act of 1981 (OBRA) provisions seem to be the factors largely responsible for changes in the caseload. (OBRA is federal legislation that restricted eligibility for AFDC benefits.) While ET may have initially contributed to a small reduction in the Basic caseload, the effect was not sustained and the caseload appears to have even increased slightly during the ET period, 1984-1987.

The second analysis examines the work and welfare participation of about 5,000 single mothers per year in Massachusetts and in other states for several years before and after the introduction of ET. This analysis utilizes detailed information on the demographic and social characteristics of these single mothers and on economic and policy factors that vary among their states of residence in each of the eight years examined. Thus we have controlled for factors such as the increase in the Hispanic population in Massachusetts, which officials have cited as a reason for upward pressure on the caseload.

The results of the second analysis are consistent with the findings of the first (time series) analysis of the caseload data. The probability of collecting welfare in Massachusetts may have been initially reduced by ET but the effect was not sustained. Similarly, ET had no apparent effect on work participation.

It is possible that some training components of ET helped to increase the employment or wage rates of certain types of participants. Thus, even though ET was not responsible for an individual finding a job or leaving the welfare rolls, it may have increased the earnings she could obtain on her job. ET may also have caused some subgroups of participants to leave the rolls more quickly than they otherwise would have. However, Massachusetts was unable to provide data on the ET program that would have enabled us to conduct the detailed microanalysis needed to establish these effects.

Studies based on randomized experiments in other states have found positive effects for some programs and for particular subgroups of welfare recipients. If such effects are present in Massachusetts they appear to be too small to affect the welfare caseload, or else they were offset by other features of ET or the welfare program that might have actually increased the caseload. For example, the guarantee of state-funded child care for ET participants while in training and for at least one year after placement in a job, plus the guarantee of state-funded medical care (through Medicaid) for the same period, may have acted as an inducement to some families to go on welfare in Massachusetts. Effects such as these, which influence the flow of persons onto welfare, are not captured in an experimental analysis, although they would be captured in the kind of aggregate analysis undertaken here.

ET is undeniably costly. Total spending on the program is projected to be about $95 million in fiscal year 1989 — more than double the expenditure in fiscal year 1986. Our analysis suggests that very little of these expenditures have been offset in the form of savings to Massachusetts taxpayers. Since ET has not reduced the welfare caseload, welfare expenditures have not been reduced. As noted, it is possible that some ET training or schooling did increase the earnings of some individuals even if it had no effect on their welfare participation. Under the most extreme assumptions, these higher earnings would yield higher tax payments that would make up, *at most,* 13 percent of ET costs.

It should be recognized that our analysis has been confined to the measurable savings and costs associated with changes in the welfare caseload. However, ET may generate other kinds of social benefits that we have not considered. For example, child care services may be valued even if they do not increase the work effort of mothers, if they are believed to improve children's development or security. Or the taxpaying public may simply wish to transfer income to low-income working mothers in the form of child care. These decisions can only be made by the public, however. Our analysis serves the role of pointing out the financial consequences of these decisions.

Some Recommendations

Although ET appears to have been managed with considerable enthusiasm, certain highly touted features of the program may have actually worked against more positive outcomes in terms of caseload reduction. One is the use of performance-based contracting, which through its reward structure encourages the placement of a targeted number of ET participants in "priority" jobs. (These are jobs paying more than a stated wage floor, typically set well above the legislated minimum wage.) As a result, contractors are given an incentive to "cream" and select participants who possess the skill and motivation to qualify for priority jobs. However, such individuals are likely to be those who would have found jobs on their own. Most studies of work programs for welfare recipients have found that program impacts are likely to be greatest for those who are less skilled, have little prior work experience, or have been on welfare longer.

Two changes might be considered. One is to develop more flexible methods of evaluating contractors that would take into account the employability of the clientele served. Another is the elimination of the wage floor for priority jobs. Employers are more likely to hire a low-skilled worker at a lower wage, particularly to start. Motivated workers may be trained on the job, formally or informally, and will experience wage increases over time. Although it is understandable that DPW would like to provide a mechanism for encouraging contractors to place AFDC recipients in higher wage jobs, the reality of the situation may be that this simply results in less attention paid to those who seem unlikely to qualify for high-paying jobs.

The voluntary nature of the program on the part of AFDC recipients is another feature that may result in less service to those who are less likely to leave the welfare program on their own. If participation in ET were mandatory and if those who are less readily employable were made the primary focus of attention, the program might spend its resources more effectively. Moreover, a mandatory requirement to participate might help to change attitudes of young women who look to welfare as a long-term option for support.

The costly child care program is an area that requires more thought. Since the purpose of these benefits is transitional, it may not make sense to place so many restrictions and regulations as Massachusetts does on the kind of care that qualifies and thus push up the costs. Would it not be better to provide smaller vouchers that could be used in less formal settings to a larger number of users? Moreover, given limited budgets, funds now used for ET child care could be spread to low-income mothers who are not on welfare.

Finally, there are broader issues to be considered about the role of a work and training program in an overall policy to reduce welfare dependence and increase self-sufficiency. Benefits in Massachusetts, as in several other states, are relatively high and may create disincentives for self-support among low-income individuals. Even an ideal work and training program may not increase the earnings of recipients enough to provide the incentive to go off welfare under the current welfare benefit system. States with more generous inclinations must, therefore, struggle with options, none of which will satisfy everyone.

The following issues deserve serious consideration:

- Should AFDC benefits be permanent for all adult able-bodied recipients, that is until their youngest child reaches the age of 18? Or should benefits be scaled back after a period of time?
- Should priority be given to making overall improvements in the schooling and training of all disadvantaged women and men to prevent the need for welfare?

Plan of the Study

The contents of this report are as follows:

Chapter 2 provides historical background on the development of employment and training programs for welfare recipients. A summary is given of the results of evaluations of these prior work programs, nationwide and in other states.

Chapter 3 describes the ET program and prior work programs in Massachusetts.

The characteristics of AFDC recipients in Massachusetts and in other states are described in chapter 4. Demographic, economic, and policy changes that could influence the growth of the welfare caseload in Massachusetts and elsewhere are detailed.

The statistical analyses of the effects of ET on the welfare caseload are presented in chapter 5.

Chapter 6 examines the costs and possible benefits of the ET program, drawing upon the statistical findings of chapter 5. These estimates are compared with those of other studies.

Chapter 7 presents concluding comments and suggests changes that might be made to improve the effectiveness of the ET program and reduce the welfare caseload.

Work Programs for Welfare Recipients: Historical Background

The nation's largest program of cash assistance to needy families, Aid to Families with Dependent Children (AFDC) was established under the Social Security Act of 1935, when it was known as Aid to Dependent Children. Unlike Social Security, the program has always been administered by the states, and funding is shared with the federal government. States set their own benefit levels and financial criteria for eligibility, subject to federal limitations and regulations.

The stated purpose of the program has always been to provide aid to children deprived of the support of a father who, 50 years ago, was likely to be the family's sole breadwinner. At the time, fatherless families typically consisted of widows and their children, and this was reflected in the AFDC caseload. In the initial years of the program, the father in three-quarters of AFDC families was dead or incapacitated. AFDC was expected to wither away as Social Security matured and survivor benefits to workers' families became more generous and more universal.

Contrary to these expectations, AFDC did not wither away, but grew at an accelerating rate, at least, up until the 1970s (figure 2-1). The reason for the father's absence has also changed dramatically from the 30s. Today, illegitimacy is the major reason cited, accounting for 53 percent of AFDC cases, whereas death or incapacity of the father account for only five percent. Divorce and separation account for most of the remainder.

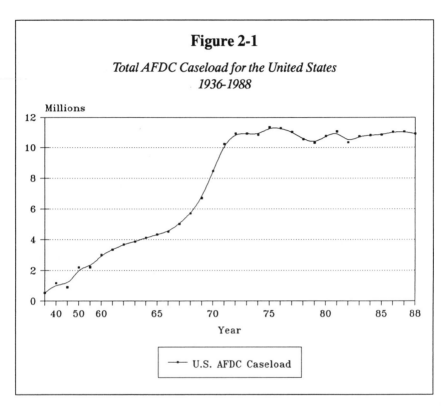

Figure 2-1

Total AFDC Caseload for the United States
1936-1988

Since 1961, states have had the option to extend AFDC benefits to families in which the father is present but unemployed. In 1988, however, unemployed fathers accounted for only 6 percent of all AFDC cases.[1] Thus AFDC has remained largely a program for families with children in which only the mother is present.

Public attitudes toward the AFDC program have grown more critical in recent years. One reason is the size and cost of the program. Although the proportion of the U.S. population on welfare declined during the 1980s, it is still, at four percent, more than double what it was

---

[1]   All but 22 states currently offer the unemployed parent component of AFDC. However, the Family Support Act of 1988 mandates that all states establish AFDC-UP by October, 1990.

in the early 1960s, before the War on Poverty. Another factor is the changing composition of the caseload, since a birth out of wedlock is viewed as a more voluntary route to becoming a single parent than the death or disability of a husband.

The dramatic change in the role of women in the economy is another important reason for changing attitudes toward welfare. In the 1930s, when AFDC was formulated, mothers were not expected to work outside the home, and few did. Nowadays, 65 percent of all women with children under the age of 18 are in the labor force. Even among women with children under the age of six, participation rates are high (56 percent).[2] The idea that able-bodied women should be excused from work may well appear to be an anachronism, bound to raise the ire of taxpayers who are themselves increasingly likely to be working mothers. Finally, there is concern that welfare may have been a contributing factor to the rise in out-of-wedlock childbearing and marital dissolution, and that children raised in families heavily dependent on welfare may not develop the characteristics and attitudes needed for work and self-support.

It is not surprising that "welfare reform" in the United States has emphasized programs intended to increase the earnings and work effort of welfare recipients with the hope that this will lead to reductions in welfare dependence.

"Reforming" Welfare with Work and Training Programs

A series of policy measures intended to reduce welfare dependency and increase self-support has been introduced over the years by Congress, the states and successive presidents. In principle, incentives to stay off welfare through work or marriage could be fostered by reducing

---

2   These statistics are unpublished data from the U.S. Bureau of Labor Statistics and refer to March, 1988.

the level of the basic welfare package or by increasing the other side of the scale — the return from work. The level of AFDC cash benefits did decline in real terms during the latter half of the 1970s and the early 1980s when states failed to raise AFDC benefits in line with inflation. However, a purposeful reduction of welfare benefits is seldom advocated in the policy arena. Instead, the major pieces of legislation affecting the direction of welfare have focused on policies designed to increase the work effort, employability, and earnings of welfare mothers.

The 1962 Amendments to the AFDC-enabling law, the Social Security Act, are credited with initiating a change in the character of welfare policy from "relief" to "rehabilitation." During the 1950s administrators had already begun to shift their attention from the enforcement of eligibility rules and regulations to the provision of social services such as child care and counseling for AFDC mothers (American Enterprise Institute 1973). The intent of these social services was largely to ameliorate the situation that had caused family breakup and thereby enable separated families to get together again.

The 1962 Amendments reinforced this increased emphasis on social services, utilizing counseling and referral services, and expanded the scope to include programs to help adult AFDC recipients become self-supporting. This new interest in work programs may have been inspired in part by the extension of AFDC coverage in 1961 to families with an unemployed father. Up to that time AFDC recipients were presumed to be out of the labor force. States were encouraged by the 1962 Amendments to establish Community Work and Training (CWT) programs with 50-50 federal matching funds. According to Levitan, Rein, and Marwick (1972), CWT actually provided little training. It appears to have been a form of what is now called "workfare," whereby participants are put in public jobs where they "work off" public assistance income.

In 1964, under the Economic Opportunity Act, legislation was enacted to expand CWT. This new law established Work Experience and Training (WET) demonstration projects to be fully funded by the federal government. The program, which served welfare and non-welfare clients (70 percent were on welfare), reached an enrollment of 71,000 by 1967. It provided vocational training, work experience, education, and day care support services — much the same set of services as current programs. Although no sophisticated evaluation of WET appears to have been undertaken, contemporary accounts suggest that the program did not succeed in upgrading the skills of trainees or in moving any significant number of recipients off welfare (Levitan, Rein, and Marwick 1972).

As has been the history of work and training programs, the seemingly poor record of WET did not discourage Congress from pursuing even more ambitious programs to encourage AFDC recipients to work. In 1967 Congress enacted the Work Incentive program (WIN), a much more far-reaching initiative than its predecessors. WIN launched a two-pronged attack to encourage work: larger scale work and training programs were combined with new financial incentives.

Two factors motivated the larger effort WIN represented. One was the growth of the caseload, which had begun to accelerate in the late 1960s. (The AFDC caseload increased by 36 percent between 1950 and 1960. It increased by 180 percent between 1960 and 1970.) The other was the rapid increase in work participation among women who were not on welfare. This employment pattern sharply contrasted with the continuing low levels of work participation among welfare mothers. In 1960, 30 percent of all women with children under age 18 were in the labor force. This ratio increased to 35 percent by 1965 and to 42 percent by 1970. (In 1988 it was 65 percent.) Yet the percentage of AFDC mothers who worked remained fairly constant at 15 percent during the whole period from 1960 to 1970 (Council of Economic Advisers 1976).

The financial incentives incorporated into the WIN program were intended to encourage AFDC recipients to work by means of an "income disregard" formula. Prior to the 1967 Amendments, welfare payments in many states were subject to an implicit 100 percent tax — a mother would lose one dollar in welfare benefits for each dollar that she earned. Under the new WIN income disregard provisions, she lost nothing in welfare payments until she earned at least $30 per month (after deducting child care costs and other work-related expenses) and then her welfare payment was reduced by 66 cents for every dollar earned beyond $30 per month (called the "$30 and one-third rule").

The ultimate objective of this provision was to encourage welfare mothers to become self-supporting. Instead, the provision became an agent for increasing the welfare caseload. It is true for women already on welfare that financial incentives to work were increased by the "disregards." However, these provisions also made AFDC available to a new group of women whose actual (or expected) earnings previously would have made them ineligible for AFDC. Moreover, the disregards were structured in such a way that women already on welfare could remain on welfare even when they worked and, in some states, earned fairly large amounts.

Frank Levy (1979) has found that while women already on AFDC might have worked somewhat more as a result of the disregards, the work effort of single mothers who were not yet on the program was reduced. This effect occurred because the incentive to go on the program was increased for higher income women, whose work participation was lower on AFDC than it would have been had they remained fully self-sufficient. Levy found that, on balance, the reduction in work effort of those brought onto welfare by the so-called "work incentive" provision outweighed the increased work effort of those initially on welfare. Robert Moffitt (1988), however, after examining several kinds of data, concluded that on balance the disregards had essentially no effect on the work effort of female family heads as a whole. Moffitt and Levy agree, however, that the WIN disregards eventually led to an increase in the welfare caseload after 1967, since the increased work effort among those already on welfare seldom led to a reduction in the caseload.

The employment and training component of WIN was much more ambitious than any of its predecessors as its goal was to restore "to economic independence all employable persons of 16 and over in AFDC families" (U.S. Department of Labor 1971). Although the program never grew to the size originally contemplated, it did grow to be quite large. In fiscal year 1975 alone, WIN program costs were about $314 million, which would be close to $700 million in today's dollars. WIN services started with an evaluation of an enrollee's "employability," to be followed by options which included direct placement in employment for those who were "job ready" and orientation to WIN and to the "world of work" for those who were not. Referrals were then made to the appropriate educational service, or job training or employment program. Child care services were provided for trainees. WIN II, implemented in 1972, added a mandatory element to the program requiring that all "employable" AFDC recipients register for employment services as a condition of receiving welfare payments. The number of actual program slots, however, never became large enough to train all registrants.

Several evaluations of the WIN employment and training component have assessed its success in reducing welfare dependence and enhancing the earnings capacities of enrollees. The results suggest that the employment and earnings of enrollees receiving services were enhanced by WIN participation, but not by very much. Among those with greater initial employment handicaps, gains were found to be more significant — a result that is often found in assessments of training programs. Despite any earnings gains, however, no significant welfare savings were found.[3]

WIN did not fulfill the high hopes originally held for it. During the latter part of the 1970s federal expenditures on the program were held fairly constant in nominal terms, which meant a considerable decline in real terms.

---

[3] Ketron, Inc. (1980) conducted a large-scale evaluation of the program. Also, see Grossman et al. (1985) and the concise review in Moffitt (1988).

OBRA and Beyond

The Omnibus Budget Reconciliation Act of 1981 (OBRA) repealed many of the changes in the welfare system introduced by WIN. The Reagan administration and many members of Congress had come to the conclusion that the so-called work incentives did not work. Accordingly, the $30 and one-third rule for earned income was sharply curtailed and allowed to apply only during a period of four consecutive months during the year. The disregards for child care services and employment expenses were capped. States were prohibited from paying AFDC benefits to any family with income exceeding 150 percent of the state's need standard (raised to 185 percent by the 1984 amendments). These changes reduced the amount of earnings a person could have and still remain on AFDC. We find that OBRA played a significant role in reducing the caseload in Massachusetts, a state that had a relatively large number of AFDC recipients with high earnings, prior to OBRA (see chapter 5). The experience in New Jersey has been similar (Barnow 1988).

The WIN employment and training program was also directly affected by OBRA, which authorized states, if they so chose, to conduct demonstration projects as an alternative to WIN. Under these demonstrations, states were given considerable freedom to design and operate their own programs. For example, states were given the authority to operate "workfare" programs, requiring adult AFDC recipients to work at an assigned job in exchange for the AFDC benefit. The state workfare programs are called CWEP (Community Work and Experience Programs). OBRA also permitted states to use AFDC benefits to subsidize a job for recipients (grant diversion). And states were allowed to mandate program participation for recipients who would have been exempted from the WIN work requirement — for example, mothers of children between age 3 and 6. The Massachusetts ET program, while not a workfare program, is one of the initiatives authorized under OBRA as a WIN demonstration program.

Table 2-1

Dimensions of Welfare Employment Programs in Seven Areas

Location	Duration of Obligation	Target Group	Primary Program Services
Arkansas	Limited	WIN-Mandatory AFDC Applicants and Recipients[1]	Job Search/ Work Experience Sequence
Baltimore	Limited	WIN-Mandatory AFDC and AFDC-UP Applicants and New Recipients	Job Search, Education, Training, OJT, Work Experience Options
Cook County	Limited	WIN-Mandatory AFDC Applicants and Recipients	Job Search/ Work Experience Sequence
San Diego I[2]	Limited	WIN-Mandatory AFDC and AFDC-UP Applicants	Job Search/ Work Experience Sequence
San Diego Saturation[2]	Ongoing	WIN-Mandatory AFDC and AFDC-UP Applicants and Recipients	Job Search/ Work Experience/ Education or Training Sequence
Virginia	Limited	WIN-Mandatory AFDC Applicants and Recipients	Job Search/ Work Experience Sequence
West Virginia	Ongoing	WIN-Mandatory AFDC and AFDC-UP Applicants and Recipients	Work Experience

(1) Includes women whose youngest child is 3 years of age or older.
(2) The first San Diego demonstration operated between 1982 and 1985. The San Diego Saturation demonstration operated between 1985 and 1987.

Source: Gueron 1990.

The Manpower Demonstration Research Corporation (MDRC) has conducted major evaluations of WIN demonstration projects operated in several states. The contents of seven of the initiatives conducted by these states are summarized in table 2-1. The most frequently offered program is job search, an activity providing assistance in seeking employment. In most of the sites, job search, if unsuccessful, is followed by placement in an unpaid public job or other work requirement of limited duration (usually three months). Some states place greater emphasis on human capital development — education and training programs. West Virginia pursued a strict workfare program with no limit to the length of participation. The West Virginia program, however, was largely aimed at men in the unemployed parent program. The San Diego Saturation program also required ongoing participation in some work or training program for as long as the person remained on AFDC, although it was not a "workfare" program. Participation in all seven programs was mandatory.

The results of the evaluations conducted by MDRC have been widely cited as encouragement for public funding of work-related programs for welfare recipients. The evaluations are based on a "randomized experiment" in which a group of AFDC applicants and/or recipients is assigned randomly to either an experimental group, which is exposed to the work program, or to a control group which is not. The control group provides a way to gauge what the work participation, earnings, and welfare use would be of the experimental group if they were not exposed to the program. Research evaluations of voluntary work and training programs conducted without the benefit of a randomized experiment suffer from the problem of selection bias, since those AFDC recipients who enroll in the program are likely to be more motivated individuals.[4] When selection bias is an issue it is difficult to determine if a program

---

[4]   Whether or not statistically constructed "control groups" can be used to conduct unbiased evaluations is a hotly debated issue. See Heckman, Hotz, and Dabos (1987) for the argument that statistical corrections can eliminate selection bias and LaLonde and Maynard (1987) for the opposite view.

Table 2-2

Summary of the Impacts on AFDC Eligibles of Welfare Employment Programs in Seven Areas

Location, Outcome, and Follow-Up Period		Experimental Group Mean	Control Group Mean	Difference	Percentage Change
Arkansas					
Average Earnings	Year 1	$674	$507	$167[d]	33%
	Year 2	$1,180	$957	$223	23%
	Year 3	$1,422	$1,085	$337[d]	31%
Employed at End of	Year 1	20.4%	16.7%	3.7%[c]	22%
	Year 2	23.9%	20.3%	3.6%	18%
	Year 3	24.5%	18.3%	6.2%[e]	34%
Average AFDC Payments	Year 1	$998	$1,143	-$145[e]	-13%
	Year 2	$793	$982	-$190[e]	-19%
	Year 3	$742	$910	-$168[e]	-18%
On Welfare at End of	Year 1	51.0%	59.1%	-8.1%[e]	-14%
	Year 2	38.1%	46.0%	-7.9%[e]	-17%
	Year 3	32.8%	40.1%	-7.3%[e]	-18%
Baltimore					
Average Earnings	Year 1	$1,612	$1,472	$140	10%
	Year 2	$2,787	$2,386	$401[e]	17%
	Year 3	$3,499	$2,989	$511[d]	17%
Employed at End of	Year 1	34.7%	31.2%	3.5%	11%
	Year 2	39.5%	37.1%	2.4%	6%
	Year 3	40.7%	40.3%	0.4%	1%
Average AFDC Payments	Year 1	$2,520	$2,517	$2	0%
	Year 2	$2,058	$2,092	-$34	-2%
	Year 3	$1,783	$1,815	-$31	-2%

(Baltimore) On Welfare at End of	Year 1	72.0%	73.3%	-1.4%	-2%
	Year 2	58.7%	59.0%	-0.3%	-1%
	Year 3	48.2%	48.4%	-0.2%	0%
Cook County Average Earnings	Year 1	$1,227	$1,217	$10	1%
Employed at End of	Year 1	22.6%	21.4%	1.3%	6%
Average AFDC Payments	Year 1	$3,105	$3,146	-$40	-1%
On Welfare at End of	Year 1	78.9%	80.8%	-1.9%[d]	-2%
San Diego I Average Earnings	Year 1	$2,379	$1,937	$443[e]	23%
Employed at End of	Year 1	42.4%	36.9%	5.5%[e]	15%
Average AFDC Payments	Year 1	$2,524	$2,750	-$226[e]	-8%
On Welfare at End of	Year 1	45.8%	47.9%	-2.0%	-4%
San Diego Saturation Average Earnings	Year 1	$2,029	$1,677	$352[e]	21%
	Year 2	$2,903	$2,246	$658[e]	29%
Employed at End of	Year 1	34.7%	26.9%	7.7%[e]	29%
	Year 2	34.7%	29.3%	5.4%[e]	18%
Average AFDC Payments	Year 1	$4,424	$4,830	-$407[e]	-8%
	Year 2	$3,408	$3,961	-$553[e]	-14%
On Welfare at End of	Year 1	66.0%	72.4%	-6.4%[e]	-9%
	Year 2	51.3%	58.7%	-7.4%[e]	-13%
Virginia Average Earnings	Year 1	$1,352	$1,282	-$69	5%
	Year 2[a]	$2,268	$1,988	$280[d]	14%
	Year 3[b]	$2,624	$2,356	$268[c]	11%
Employed at End of	Year 1	34.7%	31.0%	3.8%[d]	12%
	Year 2	39.3%	33.3%	6.0%[e]	18%
	Year 3	38.7%	34.1%	4.6%[e]	13%

Location, Outcome, and Follow-Up Period		Experimental Group Mean	Control Group Mean	Difference	Percentage Change
(Virginia)	Average AFDC Payments Year 1	$1,961	$2,029	-$69	-3%
	Year 2	$1,480	$1,516	-$36	-2%
	Year 3[a]	$1,184	$1,295	-$111[d]	-9%
	On Welfare at End of Year 1	59.8%	59.4%	0.4%	1%
	Year 2	44.0%	44.9%	-0.9%	-2%
	Year 3[b]	36.6%	39.3%	-2.6%	-7%
West Virginia	Average Earnings Year 1	$451	$435	$16	4%
	Employed at End of Year 1	12.0%	13.1%	-1.0%	-8%
	Average AFDC Payments Year 1	$1,692	$1,692	$0	0%
	On Welfare at End of Year 1	70.9%	72.5%	-1.5%	-2%

Notes: These data include zero values for sample members not employed and for sample members not receiving welfare. Estimates are regression-adjusted using ordinary least squares, controlling for pre-enrollment characteristics of sample members. There may be some discrepancies in experimental-control differences because of rounding.

In all programs except the San Diego Saturation program, year 1 begins with the quarter of random assignment. As a result, "average earnings" in year 1 may include up to two months of earnings prior to random assignment. In the San Diego Saturation program, year 1 begins with the quarter following the quarter of random assignment.

"Employed" or "On Welfare" at the end of the year is defined as receiving earnings or welfare payments at some point during the last quarter of the year. Earnings and AFDC payments are not adjusted for inflation.

(a) Annualized earnings and welfare payments are calculated from six and nine months of data, respectively.

(b) Percent employed and on welfare at the end of 2 1/2 and 2 3/4 years, respectively.

(c) Denotes statistical significance at the 10 percent level.

(d) Denotes statistical significance at the 5 percent level.

(e) Denotes statistical significance at the 1 percent level.

Source: Gueron 1990.

outcome is really the effect of the program or a result of the higher motivation of the group receiving the training.

Table 2-2 presents some of the major results, comparing the employment and welfare participation outcomes of those in the experiment with those in the control group. Results are shown for up to three years of follow-up when available. In four out of the seven programs the average earnings and percent employed were significantly higher among the experimental group than among the control group. In a fifth site — Baltimore — average earnings were higher for the experimental group, but an initial increase in the percent employed disappeared by the end of the third year.

The Arkansas and San Diego Saturation programs, which seem to have generated the largest increase in employment and earnings, also succeeded in reducing welfare payments and welfare participation. However, welfare reductions were weakly and sporadically achieved in the other program sites. In Baltimore, although the program appeared to increase average earnings by 17 percent in the third year of follow-up, this gain was not accompanied by any measurable reduction in AFDC payments or in AFDC participation in any year.

In interpreting these results it is important to note that they reflect the effects of both actual participation in a training or employment program and behavior in response to the requirements of the program. For example, people may leave welfare to avoid program participation. Also, some (from 2 to 12 percent across the seven experiments shown) are dropped from the caseload (sanctioned) or experience grant reductions for refusal to participate (Gueron 1990). On average, about half of those in the seven experiments actually participated in a work-related program within nine months of registration (Gueron 1990).

One important finding of these studies is that program outcomes differ considerably depending on the characteristics of the individuals in the experiment. In general, significant positive program effects are confined only to those AFDC applicants or recipients who have little prior employment or who are more prone to be dependent on welfare.[5] For example, among those in the first San Diego experiment with no prior work experience before random assignment, the experimentals do better than the control group in terms of employment and earnings (but

Table 2-3

Impacts of Job Search Program in San Diego, California, by Prior Employment History of Sample Individuals

	No Prior Employment			Some Prior Employment		
	Exper.	Control	Difference	Exper.	Control	Difference
Post-Program Impact						
Percent Ever Employed						
Quarters 2-6	45.5	38.4	+7.1**[1]	74.5	71.4	+ 3.1
Average Total Earnings						
Quarters 2-6	$2,115	$1,470	+$641*	$4,519	$4,641	-$122
Percent Ever Received						
AFDC Quarters 2-6	86.4	86.4	+0.1	84.1	82.3	+ 1.8
Percent Received						
AFDC in Quarter 6	39.7	42.1	-2.3	32.8	30.5	+2.3
Average Total AFDC						
Payments Received						
Quarters 2-6	$4,088	$4,227	-$140	$2,937	$3,200	-$262

(1) Statistical significance is indicated as: * = 10 percent level, ** = 5 percent level.

Source: Goldman, Friedlander, and Long, *Final Report on the San Diego Job Search and Work Experience Demonstration*, MDRC, February 1986.

---

[5] This general finding applies to at least four sites for which subgroup information has been analyzed — Arkansas, Baltimore, Virginia, and San Diego.

not in welfare use). By contrast, among the more employable group who have prior work experience, the experimental group does no better than the control group (table 2-3).

What is particularly striking about the San Diego experiment, however, is how much better those with prior work experience do than those who never worked before, whether or not they were assigned to the experimental group. Thus, 75 percent of the experimentals with prior work experience also work during the follow-up period, whereas only 46 percent of the experimentals without prior work experience work during the follow-up. By the sixth quarter of the follow-up the groups also diverge in terms of welfare use; those with prior employment are more likely to have left AFDC. Clearly, if managers of work and training programs want to show a record of numerous placements and do not have to contend with a sophisticated evaluation, they will select participants who have prior work experience (or some other indicator of employability). In Massachusetts, where managers are evaluated simply on the number of placements, there will be a strong incentive for selection of this kind.

Although the use of randomized experiments eliminates much of the problem of self-selection that has clouded the findings of more standard program evaluations, it does not resolve all of the issues. Nor can it answer all of the questions one might have about a program's effects.

The usefulness of an experimental approach lies primarily in its ability to separate out the effects of a program on a sample of AFDC recipients from what would have happened in the absence of the program. The outcomes measured, however, refer to a specific population at a particular point in time; and the results may not be fully applicable to populations with different characteristics or to periods of time when external factors, such as the employment rate, may differ. The absence of significant program impacts in West Virginia, for example, has been attributed to the high unemployment and rural character of the state (Gueron 1990). Because experiments are costly to conduct, however, they are seldom replicated year after year, or from city to city within a state, to determine how the program's effects interact with changes in the economy or changes in the mix of welfare applicants.

Another limitation of the experimental approach is that it does not provide information on the macro effects of a program that might occur if it was actually implemented on a large scale. For example, an experiment tells us nothing about the effect of a work/training program on the flow of applicants onto welfare. However, the introduction of a mandatory workfare program might deter some individuals from going on welfare, while the introduction of a voluntary program that provided services generally considered to be desirable — such as child care and extended medical benefits — might attract additional individuals onto the welfare caseload. Also, an experimental study provides no information on "displacement effects." Thus, a work/training program may succeed in placing welfare recipients in jobs that they otherwise would not have held. However, if they displace others who then go on welfare, there is little net gain from the program.

Therefore, statistical analysis, like that presented for the ET program in the body of this study, is an important complement to experimental evaluations. A time series regression analysis provides a measure of the overall effects of a program treatment on caseload trends after taking account of changes in such factors as the unemployment rate, other aspects of economic activity, and the welfare benefit level. If the work program encourages (or discourages) individuals to go on welfare, or if recipients placed by the program simply displace other workers, these effects are implicitly weighed against any offsetting factors to obtain the net effects of the program. A series of cross-sectional analyses provides a relatively inexpensive way to estimate the effect of changes in the characteristics of the population eligible for welfare and of changes in economic conditions. It supplements and helps verify the results of the time series analysis.

Nevertheless, randomized studies are important measures of program effectiveness; and those conducted by MDRC in other states should be considered useful indicators in evaluating the ET program. As presented in this chapter, the results of the randomized experiments in other states suggest that work/training programs may provide small employment gains, particularly for groups with little work experience or other signs of low employability. However, these small gains do not seem sufficient to result in significant reductions in the welfare caseload.

3

ET and Welfare: The Setting in Massachusetts

ET is clearly one of the largest state jobs programs for AFDC recipients. Expenditures on ET are expected to comprise about 15 percent of the nation's total spending on such programs in fiscal year 1989;[1] yet the Massachusetts caseload accounts for only about two percent of the total U.S. caseload. This chapter describes the operation of the ET program and its forerunner, the Work and Training Program. It then provides relevant information on the state economic environment, on the AFDC program, and on the characteristics of single mothers and welfare recipients.

The Work and Training Program (WTP)

ET is not the first employment-related program for welfare recipients in Massachusetts. Massachusetts participated in the WIN program during the 1960s and 70s. When the Omnibus Budget Reconciliation Act (OBRA) enabled states to discontinue WIN and replace it with their

---

[1]   Total spending on ET in FY89 was projected to be $95.6 million (see table 3-1). The Congressional Budget Office projected that total spending on work programs for AFDC recipients nationwide in FY89 would be $646 million (Congressional Budget Office, 1989, table 6, p. 9). Thus, ET accounted for 14.8 percent of total U.S. spending — approximately 15 percent.

own plans, Massachusetts applied for and was granted approval to run a WIN-Demonstration program. This was the Work and Training Program (WTP), which began in April of 1982 under the control of the Massachusetts Department of Public Welfare (DPW). The general strategy of WTP was to expose participants initially to job placement activities. The first stage was job counseling and individual search, using a Job Bank to facilitate placement. Those who were not successful at the first stage went on to participate in Job Clubs or more strictly supervised individual job search. Participants were given specific requirements, such as completing an average of two job interviews for every eight hours of program participation. Those who did not locate jobs during the job search phase were then able to elect programs, such as supported work or training, intended to improve job readiness and work skills. Thus the more intensive and costly programs were placed near the end of the delivery system, to be used only when the low-cost job search activities failed. Day care services were provided through a new Voucher Day Care system and transportation expenses were subsidized. Total WTP program costs for fiscal year 1983 were estimated to be $19.2 million, including $3.4 million for day care, with the federal government contributing 65 percent of the total (Massachusetts DPW, *FY84 Budget Request*).

WTP was not well received by welfare advocacy groups in Massachusetts. It was labeled "workfare" and called "an attempt to throw people off the welfare rolls" (Kluver 1985). Welfare groups particularly objected to the mandatory character of participation in the job search activities. The federal government has always required that eligible AFDC recipients (mainly able-bodied adults with children age six and older) register for WIN services. WTP required that eligible AFDC recipients not only register but also actually participate in job search activities when places in the program were found for them. Recipients who refused to cooperate were subject to loss of their benefits. The American Friends Service Committee reported that between 1,500 and 2,000 families lost their benefits or had them reduced as a result of "punitive" measures taken between April of 1982 and February of 1983.[2]

The ET Choices Program

In 1983, the incoming Dukakis administration convened a task force to design a new WIN-Demonstration program to replace the controversial WTP. The resulting plan became the Employment and Training Choices Program (ET), and it went into effect starting October 1, 1983. In some respects, ET is similar to WTP, offering many of the same activities and support services, but on a larger scale. However, there is an important difference in program emphasis, as ET devotes a larger share of resources to training and education programs as opposed to strictly job placement activities. Where ET differs most significantly from its predecessor is in terms of its philosophy and its management style. According to the Massachusetts DPW:

> The ET Choices Program is based on the premise that most welfare recipients will choose employment over welfare if given access to quality educational, vocational, job placement, and support services such as day care and transportation. The Program is designed to encourage client involvement through maximizing choices rather than to force participation through penalizing non-cooperation (Massachusetts DPW, January 1986).

The ET philosophy, therefore, emphasizes carrots, not sticks. The hope is that AFDC recipients will enhance their earnings capacity through

---

[2] See Kluver (1985). Similar numbers were reported in a study by Meredith and Associates, which found that 5,328 AFDC recipients were referred for sanctioning and 1,636 were actually sanctioned (reported in Massachusetts DPW evelution of ET, January 1986, p.8). However, DPW, commenting on the study, said that it did not have the data to verify the information.

participation in ET and then take jobs that will enable them to support themselves and their families.

Although a key element of ET is choice, ET is a WIN Demonstration program that receives federal funds, and as such it must conform to certain federal restrictions. Thus, all non-exempt AFDC recipients must register for ET, just as they did for WTP, and certain categories of welfare recipients, such as two-parent families, must be required to participate. In principle, refusal to register, or in some cases refusal to participate, can result in a withdrawal of welfare benefits. Consistent with this federal requirement, a few cases were sanctioned in the first year of the program, provoking criticism from welfare rights groups.[3]

Despite these early problems and the federal regulations, DPW seems to have taken the voluntary nature of the program seriously. To elicit volunteers, the Department mounted a high-powered marketing campaign. (Marketing expenditures accounted for as much as $265 thousand in fiscal year 1984.) Extensive publicity in the newspapers and television has featured "success stories" of ET graduates. Governor Dukakis has frequently held press conferences on ET, has included references to it in speeches, and has been photographed often with former recipients who "escaped from welfare." Videos on ET run in the waiting rooms of many of the larger local welfare offices.[4] Direct mailings (in English and Spanish), posters and job fairs are other types of outreach efforts undertaken.

The effects of the marketing campaign are difficult to determine. Possibly some AFDC recipients who would not ordinarily be well-informed were encouraged to come forward to participate in ET. Possibly,

---

[3] Welfare rights groups claimed that 43 families were sanctioned in the first year of the program, but the Department (DPW) determined that only eight actually lost their benefits. At the urging of welfare rights groups, the Commissioner agreed not to sanction and also to stress to ET case workers that the program was voluntary so that no subtle coercion would occur (Kluver 1985).

[4] The marketing campaign is described in Robert Behn (1987).

however, the advertisements, which provided information about child care vouchers and other benefits, encouraged some individuals to go on welfare who otherwise would not have done so.

Another distinctive feature of ET is its focus on management innovations. Although welfare recipients are not supposed to be pressured to join ET, program workers are confronted with a battery of initiatives and penalties designed to spur them to meet job placement goals. Each year the Department establishes goals specifying the number of ET placements or referrals each local office should attain. Monthly tallies compare actual job placements with the job placement goal. Awards are given to offices that meet these goals, while offices that fall short of their goal appear to be threatened with loss of some funding.[5] The goals seem to be defined simplistically as they refer merely to counts of ET participants who went into jobs. No adjustment is made for clients who were likely to find jobs on their own, or for clients with weak job skills who were more difficult to place.

ET contractors who actually provide the training and placement services are also given goals and incentives through the performance-based contracting system. Under this system contractors must enroll and place a minimum number of clients in "priority jobs" in order to recover the costs of running their programs. Full payment is made only if the negotiated job placement and performance goal is met. In fiscal year 1987 contractors were only to receive complete reimbursement for full-time placements that equalled or exceeded a wage floor of about $5.00 an hour (the floor varied across the state) and only after the placed person had been on the job for at least 30 days. By the end of 1988, in

---

[5] Boston met only 52 percent of its placement goal in FY89 and was threatened with a cutback in funding of one-third. Theodore Landsmark, the official responsible for Boston's program said, "the state inevitably will encourage training agencies to 'skim the cream' of easier-to-place clients, rather than take on more difficult cases." Landsmark suggested that some other local programs with better placement records were already skimming. See Richard Kindleberger, *The Boston Globe* (July 27, 1989).

some areas, the wage floor had risen to $7.00 per hour (Mass Home Care, 1988).

In sum, the performance contracting system is designed to produce good job statistics — that is, to place a targeted number of welfare recipients in jobs paying substantially above the minimum wage. The question is whether such a system provides the right incentives for improving the employment and earnings of welfare recipients. To produce good placement statistics, it would be natural and prudent for contractors to select low-risk participants — those who possess the motivation and skill to qualify for "priority jobs." But, as study after study has found, AFDC recipients with good work skills typically find jobs on their own and leave welfare relatively quickly.[6]

This problem has evidently been noticed by the training contractors in Massachusetts. In response to an investigation of AFDC employment programs conducted by the U.S. General Accounting Office (GAO), contractors in Massachusetts volunteered that problems arose due to "failure to give credit for outcomes other than placements, and failure to adjust performance standards for working with the harder-to-serve" (GAO, January 1988).

ET Employment and Training Services

Multiple services are offered to AFDC recipients through the ET program. After registration, the most usual route into the program starts with an appraisal by an ET worker to determine the client's needs and skills and to develop an employment plan.[7] Following the development of the employment plan, the client is referred to the first activity in the plan. An alternate route into ET is taken by some AFDC

---

6   See the discussion of the MDRC evaluations of AFDC jobs programs in chapter 2.

7   The time spent on the assessment and plan is usually about 30-45 minutes (GAO, January 1988).

recipients who forego the appraisal and, perhaps in response to marketing literature, enroll directly with agencies offering the chosen activity. The following program activities are offered:

1. *Career planning* provides vocational counseling services and more intensive assessment of training needs than is offered in the initial appraisal session. Most individuals using career planning subsequently enroll in another ET activity.

2. *Job placement services* are offered by the Department of Employment and Training (DET). As in WTP, both group job search (Job Clubs) and individual job search are offered.

3. *Skills training* programs offer training for specific kinds of jobs (for example, clerical or technician jobs). Some training programs are offered through the federally-sponsored Job Training Partnership Act (JTPA), but non-JTPA skills training is also available. One of the most important programs in this second category is provided by the Bay State Skills Corporation (BSSC), a quasi-public organization that develops training programs for specific industries in the state. The duration of these programs ranges from 8 to 52 weeks.

4. *Supported work* is intended to serve AFDC recipients with little or no prior work experience. Participants are placed at a work site where they receive training and counseling while on the job. The process usually takes four to nine months.

5. *Education services* are provided in two categories. One is *basic education* for those who lack the basic educational skills needed in the labor market; the other is *advanced education* for those whose goals require post-secondary schooling.

ET appears to reach a significant minority of adult AFDC recipients. The Department reports that between October 1, 1983 and June 1, 1985, about one-third of all adult AFDC recipients were registered for ET (Massachusetts DPW, January 1986). Among ET registrants, 64 percent actually participated in the program. Thus, 21 percent of all adult AFDC recipients eventually entered ET. The General Accounting Office (1988) found that in fiscal year 1986, 28 percent of adult AFDC recipients in Massachusetts participated in ET during the year

(20 percent in an average month). Preliminary findings from a report by the Urban Institute point to even higher levels of participation (Nightingale et al. 1989).[8]

Published data on the extent to which ET participants engage in particular training, education or placement services are scanty. The fact that individuals can participate in more than one activity and spend varying amounts of time on each creates a measurement problem. To properly measure participation in ET activities, a sophisticated system for tracking individuals through the program would be needed.

In their own evaluation of ET over the period October 1, 1983 to June 1, 1985, DPW officials reported that 41 percent of all participants chose job search activities, 22 percent chose skills training or supported work, 31 percent elected education programs, and 6 percent were in other special programs. It is not clear, however, whether the reported activities reflect multiple activities undertaken by single individuals or are selectively counted on some other basis, such as the most recent or the longest activity performed.

GAO (1988) reported annual data for fiscal year 1986 (obtained from DPW) on the number of participants in each ET activity with roughly the same results — 45 percent in the less costly job search or career planning services, 20 percent in vocational training or supported work, 30 percent in educational services (including vocational education) and the remainder in other activities such as participant-initiated job search.[9]

---

8   According to the Urban Institute, about two-thirds of all AFDC case heads and dependents, age 16 and older, (not enrolled in school) on AFDC in 1987, participated in ET. This proportion seems to include participation in ET in the past (17 percent participated before 1987) as well as in the next year, i.e., up to the end of December, 1988. Among those on AFDC in 1987, the percent who actually participated in ET in the same year was only 33 percent, which is much closer to the 28 percent participation rate found by GAO.

9   Although not explicitly stated, it seems that participants could be counted in more than one activity over the year.

Table 3-1

Program Spending on ET[1], Fiscal Years 1984 -1989
(in millions of dollars)

Fiscal Year	1984	1985	1986	1987	1988	1989*
Job Placement	5.1	5.6	7.1	6.9	9.9	33.2[2]
Skills Training	2.2	2.6	5.1	7.4	10.6	2.6[3]
Adult Lit & Ed	0.4	0.4	1.9	3.6	5.2	—
Targeted Population						
Pregnant Teens			0.2	1.0	2.0	—
Displaced Homemakers	0.3	0.3	0.3	0.3	0.3	0.3
Supported Work	3.7	4.4	4.9	4.9	2.8	5.0
Career Planning	0.7	1.1	1.1	1.3	1.0	—
College Vouchers	0.6	0.5	0.8	0.4	0.5	—
Support Services		0.5	1.7	1.7	3.0	2.1
Program Support	2.0	2.6	2.4	2.5	4.9	4.4
Sub-Total	15.0	18.0	25.5	30.0	40.2	47.6
Voucher Day Care	5.1	8.3	17.8	27.6	37.3	48.0
Total	20.1	26.3	43.3	57.6	77.5	95.6
State Funds	11.8	15.6	27.9	43.7	61.2	76.8
Federal Funds	8.3	10.7	15.0	13.4	16.3	18.8

(1) Excludes spending on ET for General Relief recipients (GR-ET), NPA Food Stamp recipients.

(2) In fiscal year 1989, the Department consolidated most job placement, skills training, and education activities under a single performance-based interagency agreement with the Commonwealth's lead job agency, the new Department of Employment and Training, or DET. Therefore, education and other skills training programs, shown separately in other years, are now included in this umbrella category.

(3) Reflects Bay State Skills contract only.

(4) Excludes $2.9M in Federal Food Stamp ET funds devoted to GR-ET.

* Projected. Other figures are actual.

Source: Provided in letter dated January 11, 1989, from Massachusetts Department of Public Welfare.

Expenditures are another way to determine resource allocation across activities. We would expect to find that less costly activities account for a smaller percentage of expenditures than they do of participants. Data on ET expenditures by program category sent to us by the Massachusetts DPW, are shown in table 3-1 for fiscal years 1984 through 1989. In fiscal year 1986, $21.4 million was spent on ET training and employment activities. (This figure excludes voucher day care as well as "program support" and "support services," which are largely administrative and caseworker services.) Job placement and career planning accounted for 38 percent of the $21.4 million spent, while, according to GAO, 45 percent of all participants were enrolled in these services. This is consistent with expectations.

However, the 13 percent share of program expenditures going to the usually higher-cost education activity is much *smaller* than the participant share (30 percent); and the 47 percent share of expenditures going to skills training and supported work is much *larger* than the participant share (20 percent). These discrepancies are likely due to differences in the way training programs offered in community colleges are classified. (The data on participants group together with academic offerings vocational courses offered in any post-secondary institutions.)

As ET has grown, the share of expenditures going to job placement has declined relative to skills training and education services. In fiscal year 1984, job placement and career planning made up 45 percent of expenditures on program activities. This proportion declined to 34 percent by fiscal year 1988. In absolute terms, however, spending on job placement programs increased by 94 percent, far more than the rate of inflation (about 14 percent). Spending on all ET employment and training services (not including voucher day care) has increased rapidly, rising by 168 percent from $15 million in fiscal year 1984 to $40.2 million in fiscal year 1988 and by another 18 percent in fiscal year 1989 to an estimated total of $47.6 million.

ET Voucher Day Care Services

The most important support service offered by ET is the provision of child care services through the voucher day care program. In fiscal year 1989, estimated spending on voucher day care exceeded expenditures on all other ET services combined (table 3-1). The Massachusetts DPW projected an expenditure of approximately $48 million on voucher day care in fiscal year 1989 — more than eight times what was spent in fiscal year 1984.

Expenditures on the day care program are high in part because both current ET participants and former ET participants who have left the welfare rolls are eligible for vouchers. ET graduates are assured of at least one year of the subsidy after entering employment. Moreover, if no slots are available in the state's "contracted day care system" (a subsidized service for low-income families), vouchers are continued after the one-year eligibility period has ended for as long as four years, or until a space becomes available in contracted day care.[10] In its FY89 budget submission, the Department projected that an average of 6,426 children of ET participants per month and an average of 5,778 children of ET graduates per month would need voucher day care in fiscal year 1989.

Day care costs per child are high in the Massachusetts program, due to the emphasis on formal care in licensed day care centers. Such centers must meet requirements with respect to teacher/child ratios, facilities, and teacher qualifications. Independent family care providers may be used, but must be registered and also must meet requirements. The average annual cost of day care exceeded $4,000 per child in fiscal year 1988, and for children with special needs, or for infant and toddler

---

[10]   The Department's *FY89 Budget Narrative* (p. 32) indicates that the extension of vouchers beyond the one-year period was begun in fiscal year 1986. Beginning in 1988, these extended vouchers were funded by the Department of Social Services, but it is not clear whether the associated costs were included in the ET account. Probably they were not.

care, the costs were as much as $7,000 annually (Massachusetts DPW, *FY89 Budget Narrative*). Participants in voucher day care do pay a small fee, however, adjusted by ability to pay. In fiscal year 1988, the fee averaged $22 per month.

ET graduates with day care vouchers are given priority over other low-income applicants for transfer into subsidized Department of Social Services (DSS) "contracted" day care slots as they become available at licensed centers. The income cut-off for intake into a contracted slot is 70 percent of the state's median income, i.e., $17,964 for a family of two or three. A family remains eligible for a "contracted" slot until its income exceeds 115 percent of the state's median income, i.e., $29,520 for a family of two or three (Massachusetts DPW, *FY89 Budget Narrative*).

Massachusetts spends considerably more on day care services than most states.[11] In their study of four states, the GAO (1988) noted the factors that set Massachusetts apart from Michigan, Texas, and Oregon. For one, caseworkers in Massachusetts encouraged clients to use formal child care facilities funded by ET vouchers; in other states, participants were urged to look first for unpaid care (provided by relatives or friends) before state subsidized care was offered. The regulatory standards imposed by Massachusetts were either not present in the other states or were considerably less stringent. In addition, Massachusetts was the only one of the four to continue child care funding after the participant found a job.

The generous policy of covering day care services for current and former ET participants and for providing high-cost formal day care clearly has resulted in escalated costs. Unfortunately, we lack the information that would be needed to determine if these expenditures are worthwhile. It is simply not known whether the vouchers have made

---

[11] The Congressional Budget Office (1989) provides data showing that Massachusetts was ranked highest amongst all of the states in monthly payment levels per child for full-time care for preschool children in 1987, covered under the federal Title XX program.

a significant difference in reducing welfare dependence or in attracting the more disadvantaged of the AFDC recipients to the ET program. Nor is it known whether the children of working mothers are made better off by attending the regulated and licensed day care system. Given the scarce amount of resources, however, the emphasis on expensive formal day care will necessarily result in fewer mothers benefiting from the service than would otherwise be the case.

4

Factors Affecting ET Outcomes

In this chapter we describe some of the key changes in Massachusetts that could be expected to have an impact on the welfare caseload. We look at changes in the state's economy, in the AFDC program, and in the characteristics of the state's population. To put the situation in perspective, Massachusetts is compared to other states. This information provides background for the next chapter, in which we present a formal statistical analysis of the effect of ET on the welfare caseload and on the work behavior of potential AFDC recipients.

Unemployment, Income, and Poverty

Over the past decade the Commonwealth of Massachusetts has clearly prospered. Coming out of the doldrums of the mid-70s, the Massachusetts economy started to move ahead at the end of the decade. Although unemployment rose in Massachusetts during the deep recession that started in 1982, the increase was much milder than in the rest of the country. As indicated in table 4-1, the overall unemployment rate in Massachusetts was 6.1 percent in 1978 — the same as the national average; in the recession year 1983, it was 6.9 percent (2.7 percentage points below the national average) and from that point on declined rapidly, reaching 3.2 percent in 1987. A similar pattern was generally repeated throughout New England and also in New York.

Per capita income, which is a broader measure of economic activity, also showed considerable strength in Massachusetts and in New England generally. Between 1978 and 1983, per capita income in-

Table 4-1

Per Capita Income and Unemployment in Massachusetts and Selected States

	1978	1980	1982	1983	1984	1985	1986	1987	1988	78-83	83-88
Per Capita Income										**Percentage Change:**	
(1988 dollars, in thousands):											
Massachusetts	14.7	15.1	15.6	16.3	17.3	17.9	19.1	19.7	20.7	10.9	27.0
Maine	11.5	11.7	11.7	12.2	12.7	13.0	13.8	14.3	15.0	6.1	23.0
New Hampshire	13.4	13.9	14.2	15.2	16.0	16.9	17.6	17.8	19.0	13.4	25.0
Vermont	12.1	12.2	12.4	12.6	13.1	13.6	14.4	14.6	15.4	4.1	22.2
Rhode Island	13.2	13.5	13.7	14.2	14.8	15.1	15.7	16.0	16.8	7.6	18.3
Connecticut	16.5	17.2	17.7	18.4	19.4	20.1	21.2	21.8	22.8	11.5	23.9
New York	15.2	15.3	15.6	16.1	16.9	17.4	18.3	18.8	19.3	5.9	19.9
U.S. Average	14.1	14.1	14.1	14.4	14.9	15.3	15.8	16.1	16.4	2.1	13.9
Unemployment Rate:										**Difference:**	
Massachusetts	6.1	5.6	7.9	6.9	4.8	3.9	3.8	3.2	3.3	0.8	-3.6
Maine	6.2	7.8	8.6	9.0	6.1	5.4	5.3	4.4	3.8	2.8	-5.2
New Hampshire	3.8	4.7	7.4	5.4	4.3	3.9	2.8	2.5	2.4	1.6	-3.0
Vermont	5.9	6.4	6.9	6.9	5.2	4.8	4.7	3.6	2.8	1.0	-4.1
Rhode Island	6.6	7.2	10.2	8.3	5.3	4.9	4.0	3.8	3.1	1.7	-5.2
Connecticut	5.3	5.9	6.9	6.0	4.6	4.9	3.8	3.3	3.0	0.7	-3.0
New York	7.7	7.5	8.6	8.6	7.2	6.5	6.3	4.9	4.2	0.9	-4.4
U.S. Average	6.1	7.1	9.7	9.6	7.5	7.2	7.0	6.2	5.5	3.5	-4.1

Source: Survey of Current Business, April 1989, p. 66; U.S. Bureau of Labor Statistics.

creased by 11 percent in Massachusetts compared to only two percent nationwide; during the recovery period 1983 to 1988, per capita income rose by 27 percent in Massachusetts — twice as fast as the national average. (These figures are adjusted for inflation.) By 1988, the level of per capita income in Massachusetts was 26 percent above the national average, whereas a decade earlier it was only four percent higher. Connecticut is the only state in the region that surpasses Massachusetts in per capita income, and Connecticut has the highest income in the nation.

With prosperity on the rise, one would expect poverty to fall. As table 4-2 shows, poverty rates in Massachusetts and other New England states did decline during the 1980s among male-headed families with children (mostly two-parent families).[1] Nationwide, poverty rates for this group rose during the recession and fell again during the recovery. Among female-headed families with children, however, poverty did not decline to any significant degree in Massachusetts or in other states. New Hampshire is a striking exception — poverty rates for female-headed families with children dropped by half over the decade (to 16 percent) and are now only 35 percent of the national average.[2] Over the 1985-87 period the poverty rate for single mothers was 16 percent in New Hampshire compared to 43 percent in Massachusetts.

Why are poverty rates so high for female-headed families in Massachusetts (and other states) during a period of economic boom? One reason is the relatively high percentage on welfare and the low percentage working full-time. Only cash income is counted in determining the poverty rate; and women on welfare receive a substantial amount of

---

[1] The poverty rates are averaged over a few years because sampling fluctuations can produce erratic year-to-year changes in individual states.

[2] Only a small percentage of single mothers receive welfare in New Hampshire, while the overwhelming majority work full-time (see below, tables 4-9 and 4-10). Thus poverty, as measured by cash income, is relatively low in New Hampshire.

Table 4-2

Poverty Rates of Families with Children in Massachusetts and Other States

Averages for the years:	1980-1981	1982-1984	1985-1987
Female-Headed Families (with children <18)			
Massachusetts	39.5	40.2	43.0
Maine	45.3	44.8	49.1
New Hampshire	32.8	32.8	16.0
Vermont	37.2	42.6	42.1
Rhode Island	48.9	50.5	48.8
Connecticut	41.3	41.3	40.5
New York	51.6	52.7	51.6
New Jersey	43.3	46.9	42.9
Maryland	33.3	37.6	31.9
California	34.1	41.1	39.6
UNITED STATES	43.7	46.9	45.8
Male-Headed Families (with children <18)			
Massachusetts	5.1	4.5	4.2
Maine	11.4	9.6	6.4
New Hampshire	3.6	4.5	1.4
Vermont	8.5	11.0	4.9
Rhode Island	5.6	9.1	4.0
Connecticut	5.2	3.5	2.1
New York	6.6	9.1	7.8
New Jersey	4.4	6.3	3.5
Maryland	5.6	5.5	3.7
California	8.7	10.9	10.0
UNITED STATES	8.5	10.1	8.6

Source: U. S. Bureau of the Census, Current Population Survey, March Supplements, Public Use Tapes.

uncounted income from non-cash benefits such as food stamps, housing subsidies, and medical benefits.

Moreover, welfare income is typically under-reported relative to income from earnings. No state in the U.S. pays a cash AFDC benefit that would bring a family up to the poverty line. Counting food stamps, however, the combined benefit provides an income above 90 percent of the poverty line in several states. (California, for example, would be at 100 percent; Massachusetts around 90 percent.) If other non-cash benefits are also counted, welfare recipients may in many cases exceed the poverty line.

Welfare Benefit Levels

Massachusetts is a relatively high benefit state. The monthly maximum AFDC benefit for a family of three was $579 in 1988 and $668 for

---

Table 4-3

Maximum Monthly AFDC Benefit
for Three and Four Person Families in Massachusetts

| Year | In Current Dollars | | In Constant 1988 Dollars[1] | |
	Family of Three	Family of Four	Family of Three	Family of Four
1978	337	396	584	687
1979	337	396	533	626
1980	379	444	539	632
1981	380	445	494	578
1982	380	445	465	545
1983	379	445	450	528
1984	396	463	451	527
1985	432	505	475	555
1986	476	556	514	600
1987	550	635	573	661
1988	579	668	579	668

(1) Deflated using the CPI-X1 Price Index.

Source: Department of Health and Human Services, Family Support Administration, Washington D.C.

a family of four (table 4-3).[3] During the latter part of the 1970s and early 80s, cash benefit increases did not keep pace with inflation and as a result the real benefit fell. After 1984 cash benefit increases exceeded the rate of inflation and rose in real terms by 22 percent between 1985 and 1988. The Massachusetts benefit level also increased relative to other states. Massachusetts was 22 percent above the national average in 1985 and 44 percent above the average in 1988 (table 4-4).

The cash benefit in Massachusetts, as in other states, is supplemented by food stamps. In addition, however, many families receive other cash and in-kind benefits, some of which are unique to Massachusetts. Table

Table 4-4

Maximum AFDC Benefit for a Family of Four
with no other income (in 1988 dollars) [1]

	1980	1984	1985	1986	1987	1988
Massachusetts	632	527	555	600	661	668
Maine	501	514	511	528	530	522
New Hampshire	558	488	486	487	563	541
Vermont	787	678	678	693	704	705
Rhode Island	646	501	513	543	568	590
Connecticut	735	625	628	640	629	627
New York	677	645	623	645	621	638
U.S., Weighted Average	508	443	454	460	470	462
Massachusetts as Percent of U.S. Average	124	119	122	131	141	144

(1) Deflated by the CPI-X1 Price Index.

Source: Unpublished data, Department of Health and Human Services, Office of Family Assistance.

---

[3] The monthly cash benefit reported for Massachusetts includes the rent allowance for families living in private housing.

4-5 lists the benefits available to a Massachusetts welfare family of three persons in fiscal year 1988. Also shown is the amount of the benefit to recipients, the percentage of AFDC families actually receiving the benefit, and the average or expected value to all AFDC families (which is defined as the amount to recipients times the proportion receiving it). The total average value of these benefits was $9,510 in fiscal year 1988. This estimate excludes Medicaid which would add at least $2,000 to the benefit package.

Table 4-5

Benefits (excluding Medicaid) Available to AFDC Family of Three in Private Housing, FY 1988

	Typical Benefit	Percent Receiving Benefit	Average Value[1]
AFDC Benefits			
AFDC Cash Grant	$6,120	100%	$6,120
Clothing Allowance	300	77%	231
Rent Allowance	480	100%	480
Emergency Assistance	917	31%	284
Food Stamps	1,704	86%	1,465
Fuel Assistance	565	48%	271
Other Benefits			
Crib/Layette Payments	$300	12%	$36
School Meals	520	90%	468
WIC Benefits	813	19%	155

TOTAL AVERAGE VALUE = $9,510

(1) The average value is the amount of the benefit averaged over all AFDC families whether or not they received the benefit. It is obtained by multiplying the "typical benefit" (the amount of the benefit to those who actually receive it) times the proportion receiving the benefit.

Note: The benefits shown are annual amounts for families with no earnings, and therefore exclude benefit amounts that may be received from the earned income disregard, the child support disregard and other such items.

Source: Massachusetts Department of Public Welfare, *FY89 Budget Narrative.*

Including Medicaid, therefore, the average value of the welfare benefit package in Massachusetts was about $11,500 in 1988 for a family of three. It is evident that many jobs would not be attractive enough to compete with this income level, which is tax-free and requires no work effort outside the home or expenses related to working. Even if a welfare recipient could obtain a job paying $7 an hour, she would gross only $12,250 for the year working 35 hours a week and 50 weeks a year. The financial incentive to stay on welfare is likely to be considerable for a large proportion of welfare families.

Characteristics of Women Who Head Families

The number and characteristics of single mothers in a state is naturally expected to influence the welfare caseload. Here we give a brief profile of women who head families in Massachusetts and in other states, and then sketch similar information for women on welfare.

The data that we use for the analysis of single mothers in the population were largely derived from the Current Population Survey (CPS), an ongoing national survey of about 60,000 households conducted by the U.S. Bureau of the Census on a monthly basis. We present the data as averages over a few years because statistics for individual years are subject to error due to the relatively small samples for many states.

The proportion of families with children that are headed by the mother alone has increased in Massachusetts during the 1980s. In the 1986-1988 period, 23 percent of Massachusetts families had a female head, a proportion below that of New York, but above that of the other New England states and above the national average (table 4-6).

Out-of-wedlock childbearing has become an increasingly important reason underlying the formation of female-headed families nationwide as well as in Massachusetts. As shown in table 4-7, 21 percent of all births in Massachusetts were to unwed mothers in 1987, up from 14 percent in 1978. This percentage — the "illegitimacy ratio" — is still below the national average of 24.5 percent or the New York rate (29 percent) but is about the same as the rest of New England.

Table 4-6

Female-Headed Families as a Percentage of All Families with Children, Massachusetts and Selected Other States, 1980-1988

Averages for the years:	1980-1982	1983-1985	1986-1988
Massachusetts	19.2	20.0	23.0
Maine	13.6	15.9	15.9
New Hampshire	14.9	17.5	12.7
Vermont	11.6	15.3	18.0
Rhode Island	24.2	23.2	19.3
Connecticut	18.8	21.4	18.9
New York	24.2	24.9	26.5
New Jersey	19.8	20.7	19.2
Maryland	19.9	20.2	23.5
California	20.8	19.8	19.3
UNITED STATES	19.0	20.2	20.9

Source: U.S. Bureau of the Census, Current Population Survey, Public Use Tapes of the March Supplements.

Table 4-7

Trends in the Illegitimacy Ratio [1] in Massachusetts and Selected Other States

	1978	1980	1982	1983	1984	1985	1986	1987
Massachusetts	13.7	15.7	16.6	16.8	17.7	18.4	19.3	20.8
Maine	12.2	13.9	14.8	15.2	16.3	17.8	19.0	19.8
New Hampshire	9.6	11.0	12.3	12.0	12.6	13.4	13.9	14.7
Vermont	9.1	13.7	14.8	15.8	15.9	17.2	16.7	17.9
Rhode Island	14.1	15.7	16.1	17.7	17.7	19.6	19.8	21.8
Connecticut	n.a.	17.9	19.5	20.1	21.2	21.3	19.0	23.5
New York	n.a.	23.8	25.6	26.1	26.9	28.1	29.4	29.4
UNITED STATES	16.3	18.4	19.4	20.3	21.0	22.0	23.4	24.5

(1) Births to unmarried women as a percent of all live births.

n.a. = not available

Source: National Center for Health Statistics, annual volume of *Vital Statistics of the United States* and unpublished data.

Single mothers in Massachusetts are more likely to be black or Hispanic than the total population in the state, although they are still more than 70 percent white and non-Hispanic (table 4-8). [4] During the 1980s the percentage of single mothers who are Hispanic increased from 12 percent to 15 percent, but the percentage who are black declined from 16 percent to 13 percent. The proportion who are black in Massachusetts is considerably below the national average, while the proportion who are Hispanic is somewhat higher. The Hispanic population itself is composed of groups with diverse ethnic origins. In Massachusetts, female family heads who are Hispanic are overwhelmingly Puerto Rican (84 percent). Nationwide, however, Puerto Ricans account for only about one-fifth of Hispanic single mothers, while persons of Mexican origin account for half. [5]

The educational level of single mothers decreased somewhat during the 1980s in Massachusetts, although the pattern in other states was typically the opposite. Thus, in the period 1982-1984, 22 percent of single mothers in Massachusetts had not graduated from high school, while in the years 1986-1988, 25 percent had not (table 4-8). Nationwide, the proportion who were not high school graduates decreased from 24 percent to 22 percent. The increase in women with relatively low schooling levels in Massachusetts may partly reflect the increase in women of Hispanic origin, who tend to have lower levels of educational attainment.

---

[4] Among all persons in Massachusetts tabulations from the CPS show that only about four percent are Hispanic and 4.5 percent are black.

[5] These percentages are based on calculations from the Public Use Tapes of the CPS for the years 1986-1988.

Table 4-8

Characteristics of Single Mothers

Averages for the years:	1982-1984	1984-1986	1986-1988
Percent Black:			
Massachusetts	15.6%	16.1%	12.7%
Maine	-	-	-
New Hampshire	-	-	-
Vermont	-	-	-
Rhode Island	10.5	7.9	14.3
Connecticut	28.8	28.8	20.6
New York	36.2	36.1	35.9
UNITED STATES	34.1	34.1	33.7
Percent Hispanic:			
Massachusetts	11.8%	12.3%	15.1%
Maine	-	1.1	-
New Hampshire	-	-	-
Vermont	-	-	-
Rhode Island	2.0	3.7	8.3
Connecticut	11.4	14.0	13.2
New York	24.8	27.9	28.7
UNITED STATES	9.4	10.4	11.5
Percent Not a High School Graduate:			
Massachusetts	21.8%	24.8%	25.3%
Maine	28.4	23.2	19.3
New Hampshire	27.2	19.0	18.3
Vermont	15.6	16.4	11.0
Rhode Island	35.5	31.8	20.4
Connecticut	23.0	21.5	17.3
New York	30.3	31.2	28.0
UNITED STATES	23.5	22.3	21.6

Note: Where the percentage is negligible, no figure is shown. Table includes women with children, but no spouse present, heading families or sub-families.

Source: U.S. Bureau of the Census, Current Population Survey, March Supplements, Public Use Tapes.

Table 4-9

Work Participation of Single Mothers [1]

Averages for the years:	1981-1983	1983-1985	1985-1987
Percent Who Worked During the Year:			
Massachusetts	64.2%	67.1%	63.5%
Maine	71.1	71.9	74.7
New Hampshire	83.7	81.4	90.7
Vermont	75.4	68.1	71.0
Rhode Island	54.5	66.7	65.0
Connecticut	64.0	68.8	67.4
New York	50.3	51.9	54.5
New Jersey	58.9	59.2	61.6
Maryland	71.0	74.9	73.9
California	65.6	64.7	66.2
UNITED STATES	65.3	66.3	67.6
Percent Who Worked 26 Weeks or More During the Year:			
Massachusetts	51.8%	54.1%	52.0%
Maine	56.3	53.5	54.8
New Hampshire	72.5	72.1	80.0
Vermont	67.5	55.6	58.3
Rhode Island	42.3	54.3	51.4
Connecticut	50.9	57.1	56.8
New York	42.3	43.0	45.1
New Jersey	46.4	46.8	50.4
Maryland	62.0	64.7	62.6
California	51.4	52.7	52.7
UNITED STATES	51.4	52.2	53.8

(1) Includes women (no spouse present) heading families or sub-families with own children under age 18.

Source: Current Population Surveys, Public Use Tapes.

Work participation of women who head families tends to be lower in Massachusetts than in the other New England states or in the U.S. as a whole. Thus, in the period 1985-1987, 63.5 percent of single mothers worked during the year in Massachusetts, while in the rest of New

England this percentage ranged from 65 percent in Rhode Island to 90.7 percent in New Hampshire (table 4-9).[6] The percentage in Massachusetts is about the same as it was in 1981-1983, although it had risen in the years 1983-85.

Because receipt of significant amounts of earnings often results in loss of eligibility for welfare, it is expected that states in which work participation is lower will be states in which welfare receipt is higher. As shown in table 4-10, single mothers are more likely to receive public assistance in Massachusetts than they are nationwide or in the other

Table 4-10

Percentage of Female-Headed Families Receiving Public Assistance During the Year

Averages for the years:	1981-1983	1983-1985	1985-1987
Massachusetts	40.1%	34.1%	41.6%
Maine	32.5	41.1	43.4
New Hampshire	21.8	18.8	8.6
Vermont	34.5	42.1	36.5
Rhode Island	40.8	41.0	37.3
Connecticut	36.0	30.6	34.5
New York	43.3	45.1	42.6
New Jersey	38.6	40.7	37.9
Maryland	22.4	22.1	27.8
California	36.3	32.9	33.2
UNITED STATES	33.5	32.8	32.6

Note: Includes women (no spouse present) heading families or sub-families with own children under age 18.

Source: Current Population Survey, Public Use Tapes.

---

6 The rise in work participation and the sharp decline in welfare participation in New Hampshire is hard to explain. It is possible that welfare recipients from New Hampshire simply moved across the border to collect the more generous Massachusetts benefits. However, the data to verify such a pattern are not available.

New England states (except for Maine). During the years 1985-87, 41.6 percent of these women received public assistance in Massachusetts, compared to 32.6 percent nationwide, 34.5 percent in Connecticut or the dramatically lower 8.6 percent in New Hampshire. Massachusetts is only slightly below New York, which historically has had a high welfare dependency rate. In chapter 5 we analyze the differences between Massachusetts and other states to determine the extent to which they can be attributed to differences in the characteristics of single mothers such as race, Hispanic origin, schooling, marital status, or number of children.

Characteristics of Welfare Recipients

Single mothers who receive welfare are likely to differ from those who are not on welfare. Here we use information on the characteristics of women on the welfare caseload reported by the states to the federal government. Tables 4-11 through 4-13 show the composition of women on AFDC in fiscal years 1983 and 1987 for Massachusetts and other states.

Although white non-Hispanic women still make up the majority of the AFDC caseload in Massachusetts, their representation on the caseload is smaller than it is among all single mothers in the population. In fiscal year 1987, 21 percent of AFDC parents were Hispanic — up from 15 percent in 1983. Among the New England states only Connecticut had a higher percentage Hispanic (32.6 percent). Black women were 17 percent of the Massachusetts caseload in 1987, again less than in Connecticut (35 percent) and well below the national average (40.6 percent).

The age distribution of mothers on welfare does not differ very much between Massachusetts and most other states. The proportion on welfare who are age forty and older declined a little between 1983 and 1987 in Massachusetts, while the proportion age 19 to 21 increased. Women on welfare are less likely in 1987 than they were in 1983 to have only school age children (youngest child 6+, in table 4-11) and more likely to have a child age three to five. This may reflect the increased

Table 4-11

Demographic Characteristics of AFDC Families (percentage distribution[1])

	Fiscal Year 1983			Fiscal Year 1987		
Race and Hispanic Origin of Natural/ Adoptive Parent [2]	White	Black	Hispanic	White	Black	Hispanic
Massachusetts	66.7	15.8	15.0	58.4	17.2	20.8
Connecticut	40.3	32.6	26.4	31.1	35.2	32.6
Rhode Island	74.1	18.5	6.6	66.1	17.5	13.2
Vermont	98.6	0.5	0.5	98.7	0.9	0.3
New Hampshire	98.7	0.3	0.3	96.3	2.0	1.4
New York	24.5	39.8	35.2	21.7	39.1	38.0
UNITED STATES	41.8	43.8	12.0	39.6	40.6	15.8
Age of Adult Female Recipients	19-21	22-39	40+ yrs.	19-21	22-39	40+ yrs.
Massachusetts	12.1	71.3	16.6	14.0	72.3	13.7
Connecticut	14.9	69.9	15.2	12.6	73.3	14.0
Rhode Island	12.5	73.3	14.2	10.7	73.9	15.3
Vermont	15.5	70.2	14.4	14.0	73.8	12.2
New Hampshire	13.8	74.2	12.0	11.8	82.1	6.2
New York	9.9	69.7	20.3	8.2	71.7	20.0
UNITED STATES	14.0	70.7	15.3	12.2	74.0	13.7
Age of Youngest Child in Assistance Unit	0-2	3-5	6+ yrs.	0-2	3-5	6+ yrs.
Massachusetts	36.3	22.2	41.4	36.1	27.5	36.4
Connecticut	37.0	25.8	37.1	39.8	23.2	37.0
Rhode Island	40.2	20.7	39.1	37.6	23.5	38.9
Vermont	33.2	22.6	44.2	35.9	24.0	40.1
New Hampshire	35.3	23.3	41.3	40.3	28.3	31.3
New York	35.5	22.9	41.5	35.8	23.3	41.8
UNITED STATES	38.6	22.1	39.3	38.6	23.5	40.0

(1) The distributions shown in each category reflect the allocation on a proportional basis of a small percentage of families for whom the particular characteristic was unknown.

(2) Distribution does not add to 100 percent because it excludes other, largely Asian, races.

Source: U.S. Department of Health and Human Services, *Characteristics and Financial Circumstances of AFDC Recipients,* 1983 and 1987 editions.

Table 4-12

AFDC Families by Reason for Deprivation of Youngest Child (percentage distribution)[1]

	Parent Incapacitated	Parent Unemp.	Parent Absent Divorced/Leg. Separated	Not Legally Separated	Never Married
Fiscal Year 1983					
Massachusetts	3.2	6.0	22.6	22.5	40.6
Connecticut	1.4	3.2	17.5	15.9	59.4
Rhode Island	8.6	4.2	27.3	16.4	43.0
Vermont	8.6	10.9	32.4	12.0	31.2
New Hampshire	5.9	0.0	35.7	21.8	33.4
New York	2.9	7.8	10.5	17.4	51.7
UNITED STATES	2.9	7.8	17.4	17.4	50.6
Fiscal Year 1987					
Massachusetts	3.6	3.0	15.9	18.8	54.6
Connecticut	1.2	1.3	11.8	17.7	64.7
Rhode Island	3.9	0.4	24.5	18.2	49.8
Vermont	6.5	7.8	24.5	16.0	42.4
New Hampshire	5.2	0.0	24.9	18.2	47.3
New York	3.3	3.9	9.4	22.8	57.4
UNITED STATES	3.3	6.3	15.4	16.5	53.3

(1) Distribution does not sum to 100 percent because it excludes deceased parents and other reasons for deprivation. Deceased parents generally account for less than 2 percent of the caseload.

Source: U.S. Department of Health and Human Services, *Characteristics and Financial Circumstances of AFDC Recipients*, 1983 and 1987 editions.

provision of child care vouchers under ET, which could have drawn women with preschool children (but not infants) into the welfare program. There was an even larger decline in women with school age children in New Hampshire. In New Hampshire, however, the total caseload declined by 39 percent between 1983 and 1987, suggesting that the corresponding increase in the percentage of women with children in both the 0-2 and 3-5 age groups was not the result of mothers of young children coming into the program, but of mothers of school age children leaving the program (table 4-14). In Massachusetts the caseload declined only slightly during the period (by 3.2 percent). The changing proportions suggest that AFDC exits of mothers of older children were to some extent matched by the entry of mothers of preschool age children.

Consistent with the general rise in out-of-wedlock childbearing, welfare mothers in most states are more likely than before to be unwed mothers. As shown in table 4-12, the increase is particularly striking in

Table 4-13

Work-Related Characteristics of Female Adult Recipients of AFDC

Percent Employed:	Fiscal Year 1983			Fiscal Year 1987		
	Total[1]	Full-time	Part-time	Total	Full-time	Part-time
Massachusetts	9.8	1.8	8.0	8.4	2.1	5.3
Connecticut	5.3	1.5	3.8	6.7	2.2	4.5
Rhode Island	4.9	1.0	3.9	8.3	2.8	5.5
Vermont	15.8	6.7	9.1	11.3	3.9	7.4
New Hampshire	9.3	2.5	6.8	9.5	4.0	5.5
New York	4.7	1.7	3.0	4.0	2.5	1.5
UNITED STATES	5.3	1.4	3.9	5.8	1.9	3.9

Work Program Status:[2]	Fiscal Year 1983		Fiscal Year 1987	
	Registered	Exempt	Registered	Exempt
Massachusetts	28.9	71.1	47.2	52.7
Connecticut	32.4	67.6	36.9	63.0
Rhode Island	31.3	68.7	36.7	63.3
Vermont	24.1	75.9	43.5	56.5
New Hampshire	23.7	76.3	26.3	73.6
New York	29.7	70.2	30.4	69.4
UNITED STATES	31.8	68.2	41.0	59.0

(1) Total includes a small percentage of self-employed and other categories of employment not designated as full- or part-time.

(2) Percentage distribution may not sum to 100 percent due to rounding.

Source: U.S. Department of Health and Human Services, *Characteristics and Financial Circumstances of AFDC Recipients*, 1983 and 1987 editions.

Massachusetts where in 1983, 41 percent of AFDC cases were headed by a never-married woman, while in 1987 the proportion was 55 percent. Massachusetts is now slightly above the national average (53 percent). Within New England the percentage of unwed mothers on the caseload is highest in Connecticut (65 percent).

As a result of the OBRA legislation, AFDC recipients who work are likely to become ineligible for welfare more quickly as their earnings increase. The proportion of AFDC mothers who work, which was not high even before OBRA (about 15 percent nationwide), is now exceedingly low — 5.8 percent nationwide (table 4-13). A larger proportion of AFDC mothers seem to work in the New England states, including Massachusetts where the rate was 8.4 percent in 1987.

No doubt reflecting the impact of the ET program, a much larger proportion of AFDC mothers in Massachusetts were registered for a work program in 1987 than in 1983, 47 percent compared to 29 percent (table 4-13). Massachusetts also has a larger proportion registered than other New England states or the national average. The proportion who actually participate in a work program, however, may be significantly lower than the proportion registered. (See page 34 for estimates of the proportion of registrants who participate in ET.)

Changes in the AFDC-Basic caseload are shown in table 4-14 for Massachusetts and other states over the period 1978-1988. The Massachusetts caseload declined dramatically over the period 1978-1983 (by 25.3 percent). Generally speaking, however, welfare caseloads declined more in the Northeast than in the rest of the country.

Welfare Duration

Another issue of concern about welfare participation is the length of time that recipients remain dependent on government aid. Several

Table 4-14

AFDC-Basic Caseload in Massachusetts, Other Selected States and the U.S.

Fiscal Years:	1978	1980	1982	1983	1984	1985	1986	1987	1988	78-83	83-88
										Percentage Change:	
AFDC-Basic Caseload (in thousands):											
Massachusetts	118.3	119.5	100.2	88.4	85.2	84.6	85.8	86.4	85.6	-25.3	-3.2
Maine	20.1	21.4	17.6	17.0	17.9	19.0	18.8	18.1	17.1	-15.4	0.6
New Hampshire	7.7	8.1	7.3	7.0	6.1	5.4	5.0	4.3	4.3	-9.1	-38.6
Vermont	6.0	7.1	6.9	6.5	7.2	7.1	7.0	7.0	6.7	8.3	3.1
Rhode Island	17.0	17.8	16.9	15.4	15.4	15.6	15.9	15.6	15.0	-9.4	-2.6
Connecticut	44.0	47.2	42.9	42.3	42.2	40.7	39.5	38.0	37.0	-3.9	-12.5
New York	364.4	353.2	340.3	343.5	353.1	356.9	353.3	344.4	331.8	-5.7	-3.4
New Jersey	138.7	143.1	130.2	126.1	123.2	119.8	117.3	112.6	104.9	-9.1	-16.8
Maryland	70.9	75.9	69.5	68.6	69.0	70.7	68.3	65.4	62.6	-3.2	-8.7
California	441.4	434.0	437.2	454.2	465.3	474.6	490.0	510.6	516.2	2.9	13.6
UNITED STATES	3,405.9	3,501.8	3,337.1	3,378.4	3,437.6	3,430.3	3,494.0	3,547.8	3,538.1	-0.8	4.7

Source: U.S. Department of Health and Human Services, Family Support Administration.

studies have found that the welfare population exhibits a high degree of turnover, as a majority of people (50 to 60 percent) who go on welfare leave by the end of the second year (Ellwood 1986; O'Neill et al. 1984).[7] There are no data readily available for Massachusetts on the length of time spent on welfare by recipients measured from the start of their

Table 4-15

Percentage Distribution of AFDC Families by Number of Months Since Last Opening of Case, Massachusetts and Other States, FY83 and FY87

	Total Number of Families	1-12	13-24	25-48	49-60	60+	Unknown
Oct. 1982 to Sept. 1983							
Massachusetts	91,483	30.3%	16.7%	19.2%	6.5%	27.4%	0.0%
New Hampshire	7,024	38.0	16.7	22.3	5.6	17.3	0.0
Vermont	7,280	36.4	16.9	21.6	6.9	18.1	0.0
Connecticut	44,881	24.0	15.5	21.8	7.4	31.0	0.4
Rhode Island	15,938	22.7	17.7	22.7	6.8	29.6	0.5
New York	360,372	20.9	14.2	24.0	9.2	30.5	1.2
UNITED STATES	3,571,937	32.0	16.6	21.0	6.4	23.7	0.3
Oct. 1986 to Sept. 1987							
Massachusetts	87,716	29.1%	19.3%	21.0%	6.4%	24.2%	0.0%
New Hampshire	4,329	40.7	22.0	17.7	6.1	18.5	8.1
Vermont	7,528	36.5	20.1	21.4	8.7	13.3	0.0
Connecticut	38,661	23.3	16.5	20.6	7.8	31.7	0.0
Rhode Island	15,751	26.3	13.6	22.0	7.4	30.4	0.4
New York	356,278	22.9	11.8	19.8	7.6	37.6	0.2
UNITED STATES	3,776,072	30.1	17.0	20.5	6.4	25.8	0.3

Source: U.S. Department of Health and Human Services, *Characteristics and Financial Circumstances of AFDC Recipients*, 1983 and 1987 editions.

---

[7] Because of recidivism, however, the percentage who become long-term recipients, counting multiple spells on welfare, is likely to be higher than these figures suggest (Ellwood 1986).

welfare spells up to the point at which they leave welfare. The data published for Massachusetts and other states instead show how long current AFDC recipients have been on the program. Such data are given in table 4-15 for the years 1983 and 1987. These data are snapshots at a moment in time of a group of recipients who have started welfare at different points in the past and who will remain on the program for an unknown number of additional months in the future. Changes in the flow of persons on welfare in past years and the past dynamics of caseload turnover have an impact on the snapshot and make interpretation difficult.

The distribution of AFDC families by welfare duration as shown in table 4-15 changed somewhat between 1983 and 1987 in Massachusetts. The percentage of the caseload that had been on for five years or more declined from 27.4 percent to 24.2 percent. (In terms of numbers of families the decline was 15 percent.) The group on welfare five years or more would have gone on AFDC around 1980-1982. According to the Massachusetts DPW, as a result of the OBRA legislation, the number going on the program was reduced during the 1980-82 period.[8] If the probability of staying on AFDC from year to year had remained the same, the number of families remaining to the fifth year of welfare in 1987 would be lower than in 1983, when the share of the AFDC caseload with long duration would have reflected the larger AFDC cohorts entering in the late 1970s. The Dukakis administration has claimed that the decline in long term duration is a result of ET.[9] However, no evidence has been provided linking ET to changes in the propensity to remain on welfare from one year to the next. And there are clearly alternative explanations.

---

[8] Monthly applications to AFDC dropped from 4,741 in FY81 to 4,305 in FY83 (Massachusetts DPW, *FY85 Budget Request*).

[9] The Massachusetts DPW Budget Narratives for FY88 and FY89 made this claim as did the Governor in numerous speeches. (See, for example, the article in the *Union Leader*, October 11, 1989).

Population growth, economic factors, changes in the characteristics of the population and AFDC program changes are all likely to influence changes in the caseload. The next chapter incorporates these factors into a statistical analysis of the Massachusetts caseload and the participation of single mothers in AFDC.

5

The Effect of ET on the AFDC Caseload in Massachusetts

In its budget submission for fiscal year 1989, the Massachusetts Department of Public Welfare (DPW) claimed that the ET program had placed 41,000 AFDC recipients into jobs over a four-year period and that these placements "resulted in savings of $132 million in calendar year 1987 alone" (Massachusetts DPW 1989, p. 41). If this estimate is correct, it would be a sizable reduction indeed, since total expenditures on AFDC in 1987 were about $500 million.

However, the estimate is likely to overstate the success of ET since it is based on the questionable assumption that none of the ET participants placed in jobs would have found jobs on their own. As several studies have shown, the welfare caseload is highly dynamic. Nationwide, the majority of persons going on welfare have short-term spells lasting two years or less, while fewer than 20 percent remain on welfare continuously for five or more years (Bane and Ellwood 1983; O'Neill et al. 1984, 1987). Because the flow of recipients off welfare each month is likely to be substantial regardless of the presence of a work program, it is crucial that any evaluation of a programmatic intervention, such as ET, provide for a control group or other mechanism to isolate true program effects.

This study utilizes two different methodologies. In the first approach, the AFDC caseload in Massachusetts is examined over a period of time both before and after the introduction of ET. The effect of ET on the caseload is estimated, controlling for other factors that might have affected the caseload. In the second approach, a large national sample of single mothers is utilized to estimate the extent to which the probability of collecting welfare in Massachusetts is higher or lower than in other states. The change in this probability is compared in years before and after ET began. The results of each analysis are discussed in turn.

Time Series Analysis

This analysis addresses the question: other things the same, how did ET affect the growth of the AFDC caseload over time? "Other things" are the state of the economy, demographic factors, and important programmatic and policy considerations that would be expected to influence welfare participation. The AFDC-Basic caseload (essentially female-headed families with children) and the unemployed parent (UP) caseload were examined separately, because of likely differences in the response of single mothers and unemployed fathers to external events and to ET. The Basic caseload has typically accounted for 95 percent or more of the total caseload.

An initial insight into the question posed can be gained by inspecting figures 5-1 and 5-2 which trace the Basic and UP caseloads, respectively, from the first quarter of 1970 to the second quarter of 1988. Although both the Basic and UP programs did decline during the 1980s, the timing and pattern of the decline do not suggest that ET played a major role. The number of Basic cases dropped precipitously when the provisions of the Omnibus Budget Reconciliation Act of 1981 (OBRA) were implemented starting in the last quarter of 1981. ET was introduced in the last quarter of 1983 and during its first year the AFDC-Basic caseload continued to decline, which could have been due to the lagged effects of OBRA rather than to ET. Then the caseload rose again and fluctuated up and down around the new, slightly higher level.

ET could only have exerted a major downward pull on the AFDC caseload during this period if other factors exerted such a dramatic upward push on the caseload that the effect of ET was obscured. During this period, AFDC benefits were increased and some more

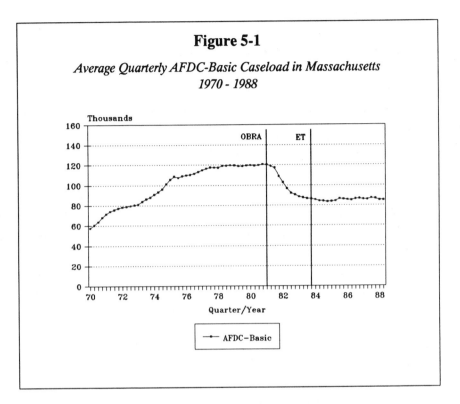

Figure 5-1

Average Quarterly AFDC-Basic Caseload in Massachusetts
1970 - 1988

liberal program features eliminated by OBRA were restored. However, the economy of Massachusetts was booming, which should have further reduced the caseload. The relative importance of the program changes and the economic boom is addressed in our multivariate analysis.

As shown in figure 5-2, the AFDC-UP caseload declined dramatically from the peak reached in the 1977-78 period. However, the major portion of the decline occurred before ET was implemented. The continuing decline after the start of ET may simply have reflected the falling unemployment and rising income levels in Massachusetts. The UP program nationwide is known to be particularly sensitive to economic fluctuations. In the following analysis we attempt to separate the effect of economic factors from ET's influence on the change in the UP caseload.

We have used standard multivariate regression analysis to investigate

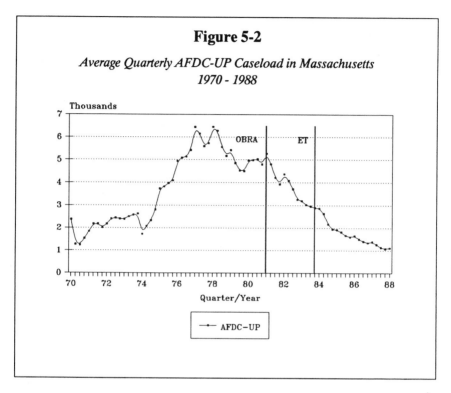

Figure 5-2

*Average Quarterly AFDC-UP Caseload in Massachusetts
1970 - 1988*

the determinants of change in the Massachusetts caseload over time.[1]
The model and basic framework have been used in other studies of the
AFDC program (Barnow 1988; Plotnick and Lidman 1987; Mathematica Policy Research 1985). We are aware of two other time series
analyses of the Massachusetts caseload. One by Garasky (1989) is
generally similar in approach to the others cited and to this study.

---

[1] Regression analysis is a technique that enables the researcher to examine the
effect of a change in an explanatory factor (such as ET) on an outcome variable
(in this case the AFDC caseload) holding constant other factors that may affect
changes in the caseload, such as the benefit level or the unemployment rate.

Another, conducted by the Massachusetts Taxpayers Foundation (1987), was seriously flawed.[2]

We have analyzed quarterly data on the AFDC-Basic and UP caseloads over the period 1970-I to 1987-IV.[3] We chose a longer period of analysis than some other studies because we felt it was necessary to incorporate the pattern of response to prior fluctuations in economic activity. The explanatory variables used in the analysis are listed in table 5-1.

The explanatory variables selected are intended to reflect the important demographic, economic, and policy factors that would be expected to have an impact on the caseload. The rationale for the choice of variables is as follows.

Changes in the caseload are likely to be linked to changes in the state's population. We used the civilian non-institutional population in Massachusetts, age 16 and older (in logs). Additional demographic variables considered were the number of births out-of-wedlock in the state and the illegitimacy ratio (the ratio of out-of-wedlock births to total births).

---

[2] The MTF study set out to examine the effect of ET on the AFDC caseload in Massachusetts. However, the period of analysis began with October, 1983, the month in which ET was started, thereby allowing no basis of comparison with a period prior to ET. Less than three years of data were included, which is too short a period of observation on which to base any conclusions. Moreover, the analytical model was poorly specified, utilizing several explanatory variables that made little economic sense. The authors admit to having rejected all models that failed to find a significant and negative effect of ET on the AFDC caseload (p. 15 of the Appendix). This may explain the peculiarities of their model specification.

[3] The caseload is expressed in logarithms, rather than in absolute numbers. Logarithms approximate percentage changes, which we felt to be more meaningful than increases in numbers of cases. The caseload data used in our analysis was kindly provided by Emmett Dye in the U.S. Department of Health and Human Services, Family Support Administration, Office of Family Assistance.

It is expected that welfare participation will rise when the income provided by AFDC benefits increases relative to the income that could be obtained off welfare (from work or marriage). The potential income from welfare is measured by the maximum real AFDC payment in Massachusetts (including the rent supplement) for a family of four with no other income.[4] Potential income from non-welfare sources is expected to be influenced by changes in the Massachusetts economy. We measure these changes with two variables. One is the unemployment rate for the civilian labor force in Massachusetts. The other is annual per capita income in Massachusetts adjusted for inflation.

The federal Omnibus Budget Reconciliation Act of 1981 (OBRA) made major changes in the AFDC program affecting the terms of eligibility and the attractiveness of the program. The effects were particularly dramatic in Massachusetts because a large percentage of the state's caseload were working and earning substantial amounts before OBRA significantly reduced the amount of outside income that welfare recipients could have and still remain on AFDC.[5] An administrative review of case closings conducted by the Massachusetts Department of Public Welfare (DPW) found that before OBRA, 20 percent of the caseload had earnings, but six months later, only 10 percent did (Massachusetts DPW, *FY 84 Budget Request*). Also, the DPW found that the state's caseload declined by 21 percent as a direct

---

4   As noted in chapter 4, the basic AFDC benefit is supplemented with various other benefits such as federally funded food stamps and state provided benefits including a winter clothing allowance and a crib and layette allowance. It was not feasible to obtain detailed information on the amount of these other benefits for each year.

5   The provisions affecting earners included a gross income ceiling of 150 percent of the AFDC need standard, changes in the treatment of work expenses, and the elimination of the earnings disregard after four months (the $30 and 1/3 provision). Among other significant provisions contributing directly to case closings were the inclusion of stepparent income in calculating the family's income and the elimination of aid to dependents between ages 18 and 21, which DPW estimated resulted in 800 closings (and 2,400 grant reductions).

result of implementing the OBRA provisions, making Massachusetts one of only three states experiencing a decline of more than 20 percent. Indirectly, OBRA may have further reduced the caseload since the difficulty of supplementing benefits with outside income may have made the AFDC program less attractive. These behavioral effects may have occurred gradually over the succeeding months.

The effect of OBRA is captured in our model by a "dummy variable" which takes a value of 1 starting in the last quarter of 1981 and a value of 0 in all prior periods. However, some of the provisions of OBRA were implemented later than others and working individuals had four months after OBRA during which time the $30 and one-third disregard provision applied. Moreover, as noted, behavioral responses to the OBRA changes are likely to occur with a lag. To capture the time pattern of the OBRA effect we added individual dummy variables for the first three quarters of OBRA: OBRA I, OBRA II and OBRA III. Each takes a value of 1 during the quarter indicated, and 0 in all other quarters.

The Deficit Reduction Act (DEFRA) of 1984 also modified the AFDC program but not nearly as radically as OBRA. Some of the DEFRA provisions softened certain OBRA changes. (For example, the gross income test was raised from 150 percent to 185 percent of the need standard.) Other provisions, such as standardizing the composition of the filing unit, tightened eligibility for AFDC. We included a dummy variable for DEFRA which takes a value of 1 starting from the fourth quarter of 1984.[6]

Finally, ET is represented by a dummy variable which takes a value of 1 in all periods from the last quarter of 1983 on (and 0 prior to that). Since ET was growing in size and expense over the period, we would

---

[6]   We did not include a variable for the WTP program of the King administration, which was in operation during the period April 1982 through September 1983. Because it overlaps with OBRA it would be difficult to determine its separate effect. However, some effects attributed to OBRA could be due to the lagged effects of the WTP program.

expect the effect of ET on the caseload to increase with time. To reflect this trend we added a variable which measures the number of quarters ET has been in operation (ET - Trend).

Table 5-1 provides definitions and the mean values of the variables used in the analysis; tables 5-2 and 5-3 summarize the regression results for the Basic and UP caseloads respectively.

Analysis of time series data is often complicated by the fact that many variables tend to change over time in similar ways. For this reason, it may be difficult to separate out accurately the impact of the different factors. Thus the estimated effects of the explanatory variables may be unstable, changing from one specification of the model to others. Despite these drawbacks, however, if caution is used in interpreting the

---

Table 5-1

Variables Used in Time Series Analysis

Variable Name	Definition
Ln Pop	Log of the Mass. population, age 16 or older
Un Rate	Unemployment rate of the Mass. labor force
Income	Per capita personal income in Mass. (in thousands, 1988 dollars)
Max Benefit	Annual AFDC maximum benefit for a family of 4 (in thousands, 1988 dollars)
OBRA	Dummy variable equal to 1 in 1981: IV and all subsequent quarters
OBRA I	Dummy variable equal to 1 only in 1981:IV
OBRA II	Dummy variable equal to 2 only in 1982:I
OBRA III	Dummy variable equal to 3 only in 1982:II
ET	Dummy variable equal to 1 in 1983:IV and all subsequent quarters
ET - Trend	Continuous variable with a value of 0 prior to 1983:IV, 1 in 1983:IV and increasing by 1 in each subsequent quarter
DEFRA	Dummy variable equal to 1 in 1984:IV and all subsequent quarters

results, useful insights can be gained from the analysis of time series data.

The AFDC-Basic Caseload

The results of our analysis of the AFDC-Basic caseload are in some respects sensitive to the specific formulation of the model and in other respects are quite stable. The five equations shown in table 5-2 all contain the following basic variables: population, the unemployment rate, per capita income, the maximum AFDC benefit, and the two policy variables OBRA and ET. The equations vary in the way OBRA and ET are modelled and in the inclusion of the dummy variable for DEFRA.

In all models, population growth has the expected substantial effect of increasing the caseload.[7] Changes in the Massachusetts economy also have the expected effects on the caseload, although the precise relation varies with the particular model specification used. Thus, increases in the unemployment rate are associated with increases in the caseload. In models 1 through 3, a one percentage point rise in the Massachusetts unemployment rate is associated with an increase of about two percent in the Basic caseload. (ET-Trend is evidently co-linear with the unemployment rate, as the effect of unemployment on the caseload is smaller when ET-Trend is included.) Also, per capita income has a negative and significant effect on the caseload — a $1,000 rise in per capita income decreases the caseload by around 6 percent. (When ET-Trend is included, as in models 4 and 5, the effect is even stronger.) The AFDC benefit has a modest impact on the caseload — an increase of $1,000 annually increases the caseload by less than two percent when ET-Trend is omitted. (The effect is eliminated, however, when ET-Trend is included.)[8]

---

[7] Alternate population measures such as the number of births or the number of births out-of-wedlock did not perform well, whether used alone or together with the broader population measure that we use.

[8] The effect might well have been stronger had we been able to use a measure of the AFDC benefit combined with food stamps.

Table 5-2

Results of AFDC-Basic Regressions, 1970:I - 1987:IV [1]

Model: Independent Variables	(1) Coefficient[2] (T-Stat)[3]	(2) Coefficient (T-Stat)	(3) Coefficient (T-Stat)	(4) Coefficient (T-Stat)	(5) Coefficient (T-Stat)
Ln Pop	8.170	7.708	8.123	8.902	8.901
	(11.399)	(15.174)	(15.730)	(19.841)	(19.642)
Un Rate	0.019	0.020	0.019	0.009	0.009
	(4.662)	(6.787)	(6.388)	(2.831)	(2.733)
Income	-0.063	-0.052	-0.068	-0.121	-0.122
	(-4.616)	(-5.373)	(-5.997)	(-8.359)	(-8.243)
Max Benefit	0.018	0.013	0.014	0.000	0.000
	(1.702)	(1.790)	(1.918)	(0.067)	(0.059)
OBRA	-0.372	-0.441	-0.429	-0.388	-0.387
	(-18.271)	(-26.383)	(-25.468)	(-23.796)	(-23.517)
OBRA I		0.290	0.284	0.261	0.261
		(8.389)	(8.528)	(9.812)	(9.729)
OBRA II		0.156	0.152	0.144	0.144
		(4.939)	(4.983)	(5.777)	(5.730)
OBRA III		0.079	0.077	0.076	0.076
		(2.494)	(2.513)	(3.046)	(3.021)
ET	-0.046	0.001	-0.014	-0.038	-0.037
	(-1.757)	(0.062)	(-0.722)	(-2.267)	(-2.228)
ET - Trend				0.015	0.015
				(5.647)	(4.762)
DEFRA			0.050		-0.001
			(2.418)		(-0.025)
Constant	-112.541	-105.621	-111.725	-122.682	-122.671
	(-10.356)	(-13.711)	(-14.312)	(-18.265)	(-18.074)
Auto correlation	0.383	0.459	0.494	0.701	0.701
correction	(2.900)	(3.050)	(3.290)	(4.830)	(4.788)
ADJ R-SQ	0.952	0.976	0.978	0.986	0.985

(1) There are 72 observations in each regression.

(2) The coefficients indicate by how much the caseload increases when the particular variable increases by a unit, holding all of the other variables constant.

(3) A T-Statistic of more than 1.6 indicates that the measured effect is statistically significant, at the 10 percent level or lower.

Notably, the dominant variable in all of the models is OBRA, which has a huge net effect on the caseload, reducing it by 37 percent or more, depending on the exact specification of the equation. This estimated net effect is larger than the caseload reduction actually observed after OBRA was introduced. Since the economy was falling into a recession when OBRA was implemented, the full OBRA effect would have been blunted by the worsening economic conditions. Thus the estimated net effect of OBRA, holding economic factors constant, is larger than the effect observed in figure 5-1.

As the set of OBRA quarterly dummies indicates, the full effect of OBRA was not felt at once, but occurred gradually over several quarters. For example, in model (4) it is estimated that OBRA reduced the caseload overall by close to 40 percent. In the first quarter the reduction was about 13 percent (-.388 + .261), by the end of the second quarter the reduction was 24 percent (-.388 + .144), and by the end of the third quarter the decline was about 31 percent (-.388 + .076), leaving the full effect to occur in subsequent quarters.[9] It is possible that the sanctions imposed by the King administration under the WTP program, contributed to the decline during this period.

The estimated net effect of ET is much less stable than the other variables and is, therefore, subject to interpretation. The largest effect of ET is found in model (1), which does not include the OBRA quarterly dummies, ET - Trend, or DEFRA. The estimated effect of ET in this model is a 5 percent reduction in the caseload over the entire ET period. The estimate is of borderline statistical significance, however. (It is not significant at the 5 percent level.) The effect of ET falls to zero in models (2) and (3), which include the OBRA quarterly dummies. When ET - Trend is added, the ET dummy becomes negative and statistically

---

9   The quarterly dummies have positive signs reflecting the extent to which the caseload, in the specified quarter, was above the eventual level reached under OBRA. To obtain the reduction in the caseload reached at the end of a particular quarter, we sum the OBRA and the quarterly dummies as shown in the text.

significant, but ET - Trend has a significant and positive effect on the caseload. In his analysis of the Massachusetts caseload, Garasky (1989), using a somewhat different specification, finds a similar pattern for the effect of ET on the caseload — that is, an initial downward effect of ET followed by an upward effect.

We interpret this set of results as showing that initially ET may have contributed to a small reduction in the caseload. However, it is ambiguous whether this effect is really due to ET or whether it is simply a lagged effect of the OBRA changes or of the more punitive measures taken by the King administration. As time went on, ET was associated with a small increase in the caseload. Again, however, it is ambiguous whether this increase is due to ET or to other factors such as the effects of DEFRA (although the DEFRA coefficient falls to zero when ET-Trend is included).

Why would ET lead to an increase in the caseload? It could increase the caseload if the services provided by ET — such as the provision of child care — were regarded as an attractive new element of the welfare package. Another possible explanation is that changes were occurring in Massachusetts, either in the welfare program or in the characteristics of the population that caused increases in the caseload but were unmeasured in our model.

The Unemployed-Parent Model

As expected, the UP caseload does not respond to changes in the explanatory variables in exactly the same way as the Basic caseload. The UP regression results, summarized in table 5-3, show that economic changes, as measured by per capita income, have a very large and statistically significant effect on the UP caseload. A $1,000 increase in per capita income is associated with approximately a 50 percent decline in the UP caseload. An increase of $1,000 in the annual AFDC benefit is associated with approximately a 10 percent rise in the UP caseload and the effect is statistically significant. OBRA is again associated with a large reduction in the UP caseload. When the quarterly OBRA dummies are added to the UP regressions (models 3 and 4), there is an indication of a phasing-in effect in the first two quarters. (The third

Table 5-3

Results of AFDC - UP Regressions, 1970:I - 1987:IV

Model: Independent Variables	(1) Coefficient (T-Stat)	(2) Coefficient (T-Stat)	(3) Coefficient (T-Stat)	(4) Coefficient (T-Stat)
Ln Pop	28.751	28.292	27.729	27.910
	(14.492)	(13.382)	(12.767)	(11.900)
Un Rate	0.011	0.013	0.014	0.013
	(1.021)	(1.144)	(1.150)	(0.818)
Income	-0.516	-0.499	-0.486	-0.497
	(-13.752)	(-10.895)	(-10.304)	(-6.692)
Max Benefit	0.096	0.096	0.090	0.086
	(3.326)	(3.270)	(2.997)	(2.577)
OBRA	-0.371	-0.383	-0.467	-0.457
	(-6.669)	(-6.510)	(-6.630)	(-5.456)
OBRA I			0.252	0.239
			(1.930)	(1.775)
OBRA II			0.234	0.219
			(1.825)	(1.682)
OBRA III			0.169	0.160
			(1.314)	(1.231)
ET	-0.065	-0.070	-0.008	-0.014
	(0.913)	(-0.915)	(-0.093)	(-0.166)
ET - Trend				0.003
				(0.154)
DEFRA		-0.027	-0.033	-0.032
		(-0.313)	(-0.379)	(-0.305)
Constant	-424.302	-417.546	-409.082	-411.646
	(-14.106)	(-13.065)	(-12.461)	(-11.709)
Auto correlation	0.796	0.789	0.769	0.767
correction	(7.056)	(6.906)	(6.443)	(6.352)
ADJ R-SQ	0.951	0.950	0.956	0.956

Note: There are 72 observations in each regression.

quarter effect is not statistically significant.) DEFRA is not significant. ET has a negative sign, but the coefficient is never statistically significant. ET - Trend is not significant either (model 4).

The unemployment rate has the expected positive sign in the regressions shown, but the coefficients are not statistically significant. Per capita income, however, is affected by unemployment, and in the UP model it swamps any separate effect of the unemployment rate.[10]

Conclusions on the Time Series Analysis

Our analyses of the changes in the AFDC caseload over the period 1970-1987 suggest that little if any of the decline in either the Basic or UP programs over the 1980s can reasonably be attributed to the ET program. Changes in the economy and in the AFDC benefit level and, especially, the effects of the OBRA provisions seem to be the factors largely responsible for changes in the caseload.

The time series analysis does leave a margin of uncertainty. ET may have initially contributed to a small reduction in the Basic caseload, but the effect was not sustained and the caseload appears to have increased modestly during the ET period (1984-1987). Since spending on the ET program increased greatly over the period, the failure of the caseload to decline is all the more surprising.

Several factors that may have had an impact on caseload growth were necessarily omitted from our time series model. The Massachusetts Department of Welfare has pointed to the changing composition of the caseload which has increasingly been composed of Hispanics and others who typically are more disadvantaged. In chapter 4 we confirmed that the share of Hispanics, of never-married mothers, and of women with lower levels of educational attainment had increased among the Massachusetts welfare population. Since these characteristics are as-

---

[10] When a regression is run with the unemployment rate as the only variable, it is highly significant and alone explains more than 60 percent of the variation in the UP caseload.

sociated with greater welfare dependence, it is possible that ET's success was obscured by a population more difficult to serve. Our second approach to evaluating the effects of ET uses a methodology that addresses this issue.

Cross-Sectional Analysis

Our second method for assessing the effects of ET is based on a comparison of welfare and work participation among single mothers living in Massachusetts with single mothers living in other states. We reason that the likelihood of receiving welfare should be lower in Massachusetts (relative to other states) in the years after ET was implemented than in the years prior to ET, if ET in fact reduced welfare dependence. Similarly, the likelihood of working should be relatively higher in Massachusetts after ET, if ET actually increased work participation.

In this approach our comparison group, in effect, is composed of single mothers living outside Massachusetts. However, single mothers are not randomly distributed among states, and women in Massachusetts may differ from other women in their underlying propensity to go on welfare. We adjust for such a possible bias in two ways. One is that we estimate the effect of Massachusetts residence in the years before as well as after ET; therefore, we have a benchmark against which to measure changes in behavior that might be attributed to ET. The underlying assumption here is that the factors creating an upward or downward bias in Massachusetts will remain constant from one year to the next. This assumption may not be true, however. To address this problem we also adjust for differences in personal characteristics of the residents of Massachusetts and other states.

The data source for this second method of analyzing ET is the annual March supplement to the U.S. Current Population Survey (CPS). We analyze all of the CPS March supplements from 1981 through 1988. The focus is on women who head their own families and have children under the age of 18. This is the population that is demographically eligible for the AFDC-Basic program. The sample each year contains close to 5,000 single mothers, 200 of whom are Massachusetts residents. The majority of single mothers head their own independent households. However, about 20 percent of single mothers live with their children in the home of a relative, usually one or both of their parents. They are classified as heads of sub-families. Because of various reporting problems the data on the receipt of welfare by sub-families may be less reliable than it is for independent families. We have, therefore, conducted the analysis for two samples: one including all single mothers (heads of independent families and sub-families); and the other restricted to single mothers heading independent families only.

In our cross-sectional analysis we investigate the effect of ET on work participation as well as welfare receipt. If ET has succeeded in reducing the welfare caseload by increasing work participation, then we would expect to see an increase in work effort among single mothers in Massachusetts. We use multiple regression to analyze both welfare and work outcomes.

The dependent variables that we use are binary variables, which indicate whether or not a single mother has received welfare or has worked.[11] Our dependent variables are defined as follows:

(1) Whether or not a woman received any public assistance income during the preceding year.

---

[11] The use of ordinary least squares (OLS) regression in the analysis of binary variables is sometimes associated with difficulties which are overcome by using alternative techniques such as LOGIT models. We ran some regressions with LOGIT and found no significant difference in the results. The OLS results are reported here.

(2) Whether or not a woman received one month or more of public assistance income during the preceding year.[12]

(3) Whether or not a woman worked during the preceding year.

The definition of welfare differs between this cross-section analysis and the time series analysis of method one. The time series analysis was based on state reports of the size of the AFDC caseload. Here, welfare receipt is based on the response of individuals in the CPS sample. It is also more broadly defined and includes welfare other than AFDC (such as General Relief or Emergency Assistance), although AFDC accounts for most of the public assistance income received by single mothers.[13]

Our choice of explanatory variables is designed to allow us to control for factors that would affect the welfare or work participation of individual single mothers in a given year. The factors generally can be categorized as those that pertain to personal demographic and economic characteristics and those that relate to the economic conditions and welfare benefits in the individual's state of residence. The explanatory variables used in the analysis are listed in table 5-4.

The regression results, which are summarized in the Appendix, are generally consistent with our expectations and with the findings of other studies of welfare participation. In equations in which all of the variables listed in table 5-4 were included, we found that black women and to a lesser extent, Hispanic women, were more likely to receive welfare than white non-Hispanic women. Never having been married, being disabled, and being younger than 25 were all strongly associated with a

---

[12] This is estimated by comparing the state maximum monthly benefit with the amount of public assistance income reported for the year. If annual public assistance income equalled or exceeded the monthly state benefit, the individual was recorded as receiving one month or more of welfare.

[13] In Massachusetts, which runs a fully state funded program of general relief, AFDC is likely to account for a somewhat smaller proportion of total assistance than in other states. General relief recipients in Massachusetts, however, are also included in the ET program.

Table 5-4

Explanatory Variables for Cross-Sectional Analysis
of CPS Sample of Single Mothers

Individual Characteristics

      Race: Black; other non-White

      Hispanic origin

      Marital status: never married; widowed or divorced

      Age: under 25 years; older than 40 years

      Number of children: under 18 years; under 6 years

      Disability status

      Years in school completed

      Migration status: whether moved from another state in past year

      Amount of child support income received

      Whether or not the individual lives in an SMSA

State Characteristics

      State unemployment rate in the given year

      State per capita income in the given year

      Whether or not the state is in the South

      AFDC maximum benefit for a family of four with no other

        income in the given year

      Whether or not the state is Massachusetts

higher probability of welfare receipt. This probability also increased substantially as the number of children increased, especially children under the age of six. The probability of receiving welfare fell sharply as schooling increased, and it fell as the amount of child support increased. Welfare receipt was generally higher in states with high welfare benefit levels and high unemployment, though the coefficients on these variables were not statistically significant in all years. In states with higher per capita income and states in the South, welfare receipt was lower.

The results of our analysis of the probability of working were consistent with the welfare receipt regressions. Work participation is usually low among women on welfare since high earnings typically preclude eligibility for welfare receipt. Therefore, we expect that variables which have a positive effect on welfare receipt (such as the number of children under age 6) will have a negative effect on the probability of working. And that is what we found.

The variable that is the primary focus of our interest is a dummy variable indicating whether or not the individual woman is a resident of Massachusetts. The coefficient of this variable shows the percentage point difference in the probability of welfare receipt (or work participation) between Massachusetts and all other states, *net* of the effects of: 1) differences in the measured characteristics of Massachusetts residents and residents of other states, and 2) economic and program differences between states. (The differences in characteristics and economic conditions are captured by the other explanatory variables.) Tables 5-5 through 5-7 show the "Massachusetts effect" for each dependent variable, for the years 1980-1987 and for the two alternate samples of single mothers.

In most years, including the ET years of 1985-87, the Massachusetts effect is positive and significant with respect to welfare receipt. For example, in 1987, the fourth year of ET, the probability of receiving one month or more of welfare is ten percentage points higher in Massachusetts than in other states. This is a larger effect than in 1981 before ET existed.

There is a period of two years — 1983 and 1984 — when the Massachusetts effect all but disappears and the probability of welfare receipt is not significantly higher in Massachusetts than in other states (for women with similar characteristics). It seems unlikely that ET could be responsible for much of the relative fall in welfare receipt in 1983, since ET did not start until October of 1983 and the welfare measure is defined quite loosely, as one month or more of welfare receipt during the year (or any welfare receipt during the year). But 1984 is the first full year of ET's operation, and the relatively low level of welfare receipt in Massachusetts in that year could be attributed to ET. Even at the low points of 1983 and 1984, however, the probability of collecting welfare among single mothers in Massachusetts never fell below the level of the other states. If indeed ET was responsible for the decline in welfare in 1984 (and part of 1983), the effect was not

Table 5-5

Probability of Receiving One Month or More of Public Assistance During the Year: Percentage Point Difference Between Massachusetts and All Other States

	Sample I Female heads of families[1]	Sample II Female heads of families and sub-families[1,2]
1980	+ 16.2 ***[3]	+ 15.6 ***
1981	+ 8.6 **	+ 10.4 ***
1982	+ 7.7 *	+ 11.7 ***
1983	+ 1.5	+ 1.4
1984	+ 2.1	+ 1.8
1985	+ 7.4 **	+ 8.4 ***
1986	+ 9.8 ***	+ 10.8 ***
1987	+ 10.1 ***	+ 10.1 ***

(1) Restricted to women with own children under age 18 as reported in March of the following year.

(2) Both related and unrelated heads of sub-families are included.

(3) Starred figures denote that the differential is statistically significant at the following levels: *   10 percent level

               **   5 percent level

               ***   1 percent level

Source: Derived from multiple regression analysis of a sample of approximately 5,000 individual female family heads in the Current Population Survey each year. See text and appendix for details.

sustained, as single mothers in Massachusetts again became significantly more likely to collect welfare in Massachusetts than elsewhere.

In seeking to explain the pattern of change from year to year in the Massachusetts effect, it is important to recognize that federal legislation such as OBRA and DEFRA were applied to all of the states. In our time series analysis we found that OBRA sharply reduced the caseload in Massachusetts starting in the last quarter of 1981. This reduction in the caseload would only show up as a reduction in the Massachusetts effect in our cross-sectional analysis, if OBRA reduced the caseload

Table 5-6

Probability of Receiving Any Public Assistance During the Year: Percentage Point Difference Between Massachusetts and All Other States

	Sample I Female heads of families[1]	Sample II Female heads of families and sub-families[1,2]
1980	+14.3	+13.9 ***
1981	+9.3 **[3]	+11.7 ***
1982	+9.1 *	+12.4 ***
1983	+1.6	+ 1.9
1984	+1.9	+ 2.1
1985	+6.9 **	+ 7.4 **
1986	+10.1 ***	+11.1 ***
1987	+9.4 ***	+9.7 ***

(1) Restricted to women with own children under age 18 as reported in March of the following year.

(2) Both related and unrelated heads of sub-families are included.

(3) Starred figures denote that the differential is statistically significant at the following levels:
         *   10 percent level
        **   5 percent level
      *** 1 percent level

more in Massachusetts than in other states among similarly situated women (with respect to their personal and environmental characteristics). This does not seem to have happened in 1982, but it is possible that the effect of OBRA was deeper and more lasting in Massachusetts and that this contributed to the reduced likelihood of receiving welfare in 1983 and 1984.

The probability of working during the year is also subject to a Massachusetts effect. In this case (table 5-7), single mothers in Massachusetts are less likely to work than are single mothers in other states, although the effect is negligible and statistically insignificant in the years 1982-1984. The results are generally the flip side of the welfare results.

In interpreting these results we reviewed the possible factors that

Table 5-7

Probability of Working During the Year: Percentage Point Difference Between Massachusetts and All Other States

	Sample I Female heads of families[1]	**Sample II** Female heads of families and sub-families[1,2]
1980	-4.4	-3.4
1981	-8.7 **[3]	-8.8 **
1982	-4.1	-4.4
1983	-2.7	+0.2
1984	-1.6	-1.1
1985	-8.0 **	-7.3 **
1986	-6.8 **	-5.4 *
1987	-5.7 *	-5.6 *

(1) Restricted to women with own children under age 18 as reported in March of the following year.

(2) Both related and unrelated heads of sub-families are included.

(3) Starred figures denote that the differential is statistically significant at the following levels: *   10 percent level
                                **   5 percent level
                              ***   1 percent level

were necessarily omitted from our analysis and that might explain why ET failed to reduce the Massachusetts effect on welfare or work participation in the 1985-87 period. Our cross-sectional analysis does control for changes in the race and Hispanic origin of single mothers and for schooling and other factors that influence welfare receipt. However, it is possible that ethnicity and race interact with other variables in such a way as to influence the outcome. To adjust further for compositional effects and interactions, we conducted additional analysis of the more homogeneous population of white non-Hispanic single mothers. The resulting Massachusetts coefficients are reported in table 5-8 and the full regressions in the Appendix.

The pattern of change in the coefficients for white non-Hispanic

Table 5-8

Welfare Receipt and Work Participation Among White Non-Hispanic Women Heading Families: Percentage Point Difference Between Massachusetts and All Other States[1]

	Probability of Receiving One Month or More of Public Assistance	Probability of Working During the Year
1980	+15.0 ***[2]	-4.7
1981	+ 4.8	-3.1
1982	+ 5.6	-4.6
1983	+ 2.8	-3.2
1984	- 1.6	+1.2
1985	+ 9.8 ***	-8.9 ***
1986	+ 4.9	-2.5
1987	+11.9 ***	-5.4

(1) Restricted to female heads of primary families with own children under the age of 18, as reported in March of the following year. Only white non-Hispanic women are included.

(2) Starred figures denote that the differential is statistically significant at the following levels:

	*	10 percent level
	**	5 percent level
	***	1 percent level

women is similar to the results for the whole sample. However, the probability of collecting welfare is both positive and significantly higher in Massachusetts than it is in other states only in 1980, and then again in the ET years of 1985 and 1987. Again we find no lasting impact of ET in reducing welfare participation. With respect to the likelihood of working, the Massachusetts coefficient is negative and significant among white non-Hispanic women only in the ET year of 1985. In most of the other years this coefficient is also negative but it is not significant. The information is not sufficient to conclude that ET reduced work participation, but it clearly suggests that ET has not increased the work effort of white non-Hispanic single mothers.

Due to the lack of data, we could not include detailed measures of the characteristics of state welfare and work programs for all of the states. Some states are much stricter than others in their interpretation of regulations and in their administration of the AFDC program. States also vary in the extent to which benefits are provided in addition to the basic cash and food stamp benefits. Presumably Massachusetts is a state that is more generous and more lenient, and this is why there is a Massachusetts effect. ET does not seem to have provided a mechanism for countering these forces. It is improbable that the existence of superior work programs in the other states can account for the Massachusetts effect. Although other states also have had work programs, few if any have been nearly as large as Massachusetts' in terms of dollars spent per AFDC recipient.

6

The Bottom Line: Costs and Benefits

Ultimately the question to be answered is whether ET has been a worthwhile expenditure for taxpayers as well as for recipients. In this chapter we utilize our findings on the impact of ET to assess the net costs and savings to the taxpayer. After examining the costs and benefits of ET we compare our results with those of the Massachusetts Department of Public Welfare.

A standard procedure for evaluating government programs is to compare the value of the program's benefits with its costs. From the perspective of the taxpayer, the gross benefits from the ET program would depend on the extent to which transfer payments were reduced and tax revenues were increased. Thus, ET could produce taxpayer benefits if it caused the earnings and employment of AFDC recipients to rise and if this rise in income in turn led to a reduction in welfare benefits and an increase in the taxes paid by ET graduates. The actual net gain to taxpayers depends on the extent to which the gross benefits attributable to ET exceed the costs of the program.[1]

---

[1] From the perspective of ET participants, a net gain would be realized if the earnings gain attributable to ET exceeded the loss of AFDC benefits and increased tax payments and work expenses. From the perspective of society as a whole, the net benefit is a weighted sum of the net benefits to both taxpayers and participants. In this study we focus primarily on the net benefit to taxpayers since that has been the focus of much of the public discussion about this program.

Table 6-1

Cost Data for ET, Fiscal Years 1984 - 1989

Fiscal Years:	1984	1985	1986	1987	1988	1989*
Total expenditures:						
Current dollars (millions)	$20.1	26.3	43.3	57.6	77.5	95.6
FY89 dollars (millions)	$23.4	29.5	47.7	61.2	79.2	95.6
New Participants[1]	15,600	19,681	26,637	33,045	38,026	n.a.[2]
Placements	6,040	11,089	12,870	9,898	13,075	14,028[3]
Expenditures per participant (FY89 dollars)	$1,500	1,499	1,791	1,852	2,083	n.a.
Expenditures per placement (FY89 dollars)	$3,874	2,660	3,706	6,183	6,057	6,815

(1) This is the number of new participants in the program each month, summed over the twelve months in the fiscal year.

(2) n.a. = not available

(3) Estimated based on the difference between the number of placements during the 5-year period FY84-FY88 and the number of placements for the 6-year period including FY89 announced by the Governor in October, 1989 (67,000 placements).

* Projected

Source: Massachusetts Department of Public Welfare.

The costs of the ET program have been considerable. As indicated in table 6.1, total expenditures cumulated over the six-year period — fiscal years 1984-89 — were $320.4 million, or $336.6 million when expressed in 1989 dollars. The trend in annual costs has been upwards as program expenditures totalled $95.6 million in fiscal year 1989, reflecting a 218 percent rise above the level of fiscal year 1985, the first full year of the program.

The costs of ET per participant appear to be considerably above the level of spending of most other states that run employment and training programs for welfare recipients. In fiscal year 1988, Massachusetts spent approximately $2,000 per ET participant, up from $1,500 in fiscal year 1985 (table 6.1).[2] Among the state programs evaluated by the Manpower Demonstration Research Corporation (MDRC), gross costs per participant were about $430 in Arkansas, the lowest cost state, and averaged $600 per participant in the well-known first San Diego program.[3] Only Maryland was close to Massachusetts in costs, spending about $1,800 per participant in fiscal year 1984.

In its study of programs in four states, including Massachusetts, the General Accounting Office (GAO) using a different definition of par-

---

[2] The Massachusetts DPW would only provide us with data on the number of participants entering ET each month. These data were summed over the 12-month period to obtain annual participant totals. The measure is not ideal as it is influenced by changes in the duration of time spent in ET. It may also be subject to double counting if individuals enter ET more than once during the year.

[3] These cost data are obtained from the various state reports issued by the MDRC. MDRC presents total costs over the course of the program per individual who was part of the experiment. However, in most states only about half of the experimentals actually participated in work-related programs. To put the costs on a roughly comparable basis with participant costs for Massachusetts, we multiplied costs per experimental by the inverse of the proportion participating.

ticipants, found that expenditures per participant in Massachusetts were $1,257 in 1986, compared to $410 in Michigan and $170 in Texas.[4] (No participant data were available for Oregon, the fourth state.) As discussed in chapter 3, the higher program costs in Massachusetts (and in Maryland) in part reflect a greater emphasis on education and training programs, which are typically more expensive than other work-related programs such as job search. The relative costliness of the child care program in Massachusetts is another important reason for its higher overall expenditures.

The extent to which the ET program has been cost-effective for Massachusetts taxpayers depends on the extent to which the savings generated by the program exceed the costs. The two possible sources of these savings would be: 1) reductions in transfer payments to AFDC recipients whose employment or earnings were increased as a result of exposure to ET and who as a result left the caseload or received a lower welfare benefit; and 2) increases in taxes paid by those individuals whose earnings were increased by ET.

In this study we have conducted a detailed investigation of the effects of ET on welfare participation and employment status. Our results, which are discussed at length in chapter 5, indicate that ET has not had any significant impact on welfare or employment participation in Massachusetts. Since virtually no case closings can reasonably be attributed to ET, there are no savings to taxpayers from this source.[5]

Another potential source of savings would be any reductions in welfare payments to recipients whose earnings were increased by ET but not enough to generate a case closing. This could not be a major

---

[4]   The GAO data on participants referred to the number of participants for the entire year, which includes participants already in ET at the beginning of the year. Our data refer only to new participants in ET.

[5]   Indeed, our time series analysis of the AFDC caseload in Massachusetts suggests that ET actually had the effect of increasing the caseload somewhat. We took the conservative approach, however, and considered the effect of ET to be zero.

source of savings since the amount of income welfare recipients can earn and still remain on the program has been sharply restricted since the implementation of the OBRA amendments. As noted in chapter 5, the OBRA changes reduced by half the percentage of AFDC recipients with earnings in Massachusetts. In fiscal year 1983, after OBRA but prior to ET, 9.8 percent of adult AFDC recipients had earnings in Massachusetts. In fiscal year 1987 this percentage was even lower — 8.4 percent (see table 4-13). It does not seem likely that ET resulted in any substantial increase in earnings or reductions in benefit payments among this small category of AFDC recipients.

The last potential source of savings gains from ET are the additional taxes paid by former welfare recipients whose earnings were increased by ET. Even if most AFDC recipients who found jobs would have done so anyway (without ET), it is possible that ET training and education programs increased skills and thereby increased the wage rates these people could obtain when they worked. The MDRC evaluation of the Maryland jobs program found that it had no effect on the extent of welfare receipt although it did have the effect of increasing the earnings of participants. This earnings gain amounted to $1,000 per person in the experiment, accumulated over quarters 2-12 after the initial assignment to the program.

An earnings increase can occur either through an increase in weeks and hours worked, or by an increase in hourly wage rates. We found that ET has had no positive impact on the probability of working (or on weeks worked).[6] Due to lack of relevant data we could not estimate the effect of ET on the wage rates of participants. However, we can estimate an upper bound to the earnings increase that could possibly be attributed to ET and from that, derive the additional tax payments that would be made as a result of the higher earnings. To obtain such

---

[6]   See chapter 5 and the Appendix for the analysis of the effect of ET on the employment status of single mothers. A similar analysis was conducted on weeks worked. The results were similar — the number of weeks worked was not increased by ET.

an upper limit estimate we make the unlikely assumption that each of the ET graduates the Dukakis administration claims to have placed during the fiscal year 1984-1988 period (52,972 persons) received, or will receive, a gain in earnings of $3,000 over a period of time. This is triple the gain in earnings estimated for a comparable period of time for the Maryland program. Such a gain at most would generate additional federal and state tax payments of $600 per placement (assuming a combined tax rate of 20 percent). ET costs *per placement*, however, averaged $4,550 during the fiscal year 1984-1988 period. Thus, under the most extreme assumptions favorable to ET, the increased tax payments of ET graduates would offset only 13 percent of the program costs. Under more plausible assumptions, the offset would be substantially smaller.

In sum, total expenditures on ET from fiscal year 1984 to 1988 cumulated to $241 million. We estimate that there were no offsetting savings to taxpayers from reduced welfare payments, since ET had no effect on case closings or the probability of working. The one possible source of savings is increased tax payments made by those ET graduates who, although they would have found jobs on their own without ET, may have experienced an increase in their wage rates due to skills obtained in ET. We did not have the data to analyze this effect and, therefore, cannot reject the possibility of savings from this source. However, under extreme assumptions, the most that could be expected from this source would be $31 million, or 13 percent of total program costs. Thus, the net cost of ET to taxpayers was $210 million over the 5-year period, fiscal years 1984-1988. Most of this cost (71 percent) was borne by Massachusetts taxpayers exclusively. The remainder came from federal funds to which Massachusetts taxpayers also contributed.

Other Estimates of ET Net Savings

In September of 1989 the Dukakis administration claimed that it had placed more than 67,000 welfare recipients and applicants into jobs through ET since the inception of the program in October of 1983. The claim was also made that "after deducting the cost of the program, ET saved over $280 million, through the end of fiscal year 1988, in reduced welfare benefits and increased revenues from Social Security contributions and income and sales taxes" (Massachusetts DPW, September 1989). Claims such as these have been regularly made by the Massachusetts DPW and have been widely publicized by the Governor.

How can the DPW find that ET has saved the taxpayers $280 million, while we find that ET has cost the taxpayers at least $210 million? DPW has not provided any evidence or analysis to back up their assertions. In fact, the only explanation we could find for their estimate of net savings appeared in a short paragraph in the Department's budget submission for FY87 and refers to the first two years of ET. The paragraph reads as follows:

> Since October 1, 1983 more than 23,000 AFDC recipients have been placed into full or part-time jobs at a total cost of $71 million. The average cost per ET placement is therefore approximately $3,100. The typical AFDC case in Massachusetts costs $6,100 per year — $4,800 in a cash grant and $1,300 in Medicaid services. The cost of maintaining 23,000 AFDC cases for a single year would therefore total $140 million. Thus, by placing 23,000 recipients into jobs, ET has saved some $69 million. In FY87, net ET savings will be $30 million (Massachusetts DPW, January 22, 1986).

There are several errors in this calculation. The two major ones are the implicit assumptions that: 1) all of the 23,000 AFDC recipients who found jobs while in the ET program would not have found jobs on their own; and 2) that all of the job finders left the caseload. As we have repeatedly stressed, ET can only be credited with achieving savings if it produces a positive outcome that would not have occurred in the absence of the program. For example, the AFDC caseload has always been highly dynamic in Massachusetts, just as it has been nationwide, with a large number of case closings each month. In fiscal year 1983, before ET was in place, case closings were reported to have averaged 4,000 per month. The same statistic is reported for the years after ET began. Moreover, the proportion of cases closed because the head of the family found a job was 52 percent in fiscal year 1983 and only 48 percent in the ET era (broken down into 32 percent finding jobs on their own and 18 percent finding jobs through ET).[7]

To determine the extent to which ET is responsible for employment gains or case closings, it is clearly necessary to utilize an evaluation scheme that incorporates a control mechanism. Findings from the randomized experiments conducted by MDRC provide vivid evidence of the extent to which a program's effectiveness can be grossly overstated by focusing on job placements without reference to a control. For example, among those assigned to the experimental group in San Diego's Job Search-Community Work Experience Program (CWEP) over 60 percent found jobs during the second through sixth quarters of the follow-up period. As Judith Gueron, director of the MDRC demonstrations, comments:

> If one assumes that all of this employment was caused by the program — and multiplies the number of placements or employed individuals by the average reduction in grant payments that takes place after employment — the result is extremely large welfare savings. Instead, [the data] reveal that over 55 percent of the controls worked at some time during the same period *without* participating in the Job Search-CWEP program. The real gain for experimentals is still notable — around 6 percentage points — but is much more modest. Unfortunately, most program administrators only have data on program participants and not on a control group. Thus, while it will be tempting for them to look at

---

[7]   For the data on case closings in fiscal year 1983 see Massachusetts DPW, January 13, 1984, and for the reasons for case closings in fiscal year 1983 see Massachusetts DPW, February 1987. For the data on case closings and the reasons for them in the ET era, see Massachusetts DPW, February 13, 1987 and *FY89 Budget Narrative.*

operational data and assume that all changes are program achievements, the data from this demonstration suggest how misleading this can be (Gueron 1986).

No randomized experiment has been conducted in Massachusetts. In order to isolate net program effects, we used various procedures for establishing a counterfactual situation or a comparison group. We found no significant effect of ET on welfare participation or employment. DPW has used gross placement data for evaluating the success of ET and has not tried to determine how many of the persons placed would have found jobs and left the caseload on their own. As a result they have concluded that ET has been highly successful in producing welfare savings. Our analysis demonstrates that this conclusion is wrong.

The Urban Institute Study

Recently the Urban Institute released preliminary findings from a study of the ET program commissioned by the Massachusetts DPW (Nightingale et al. 1989). The Urban Institute study does not provide a means for evaluating the success of ET in reducing the AFDC caseload. This was evidently not the purpose of the study and no comparison group was provided that would enable any judgments to be formed on the overall effectiveness of the program.[8] Instead, the preliminary findings largely present descriptive information about the proportion of AFDC recipients who had contact with ET and the proportion of ET participants who ultimately found jobs. As with the DPW data on job placements, this kind of information presented without a basis of comparison says nothing about the effectiveness of ET.

---

[8] The major aim of the study is to compare the effectiveness of one type of ET program treatment with another, for example, JTPA skills training with job search.

The Urban Institute report has been cited as showing that the extension of ET child care subsidies and Medicaid health benefits for a 12-month transition period was important in helping welfare parents retain their jobs (e.g., Armstrong 1989). However, this is not a conclusion that can be drawn from the study. Since everyone in the study sample was eligible for subsidized child care and health benefits whether or not they used the benefits, there is no way to test for the effect of the availability of child care subsidies on work patterns. The study finds a positive statistical association between steady child care arrangements and job retention. However, this association is likely to reflect the fact that mothers of small children who seriously plan to continue working are more likely to take the trouble to make child care arrangements than those who do not plan to work for long.

The availability of subsidized child care may in fact influence the work patterns of mothers. To measure this effect, however, one would need a mechanism to compare the work patterns of mothers with the same propensity to work but with varying *availability* of day care. The Urban Institute's preliminary findings present interesting facts about ET but cannot be used to estimate the net benefits of the ET program.

Benefits to Participants

Even though ET did not produce a net benefit to the taxpayer, it is possible that the program did benefit those welfare recipients who participated in the various types of employment and training programs offered. Programs in basic education, vocational training and guided job search may well enhance earnings. Moreover, the direct costs to the participants are minimal, as child care and even transportation are subsidized. However, without access to detailed data on program participants and outcomes and a way of constructing an appropriate control group we could not determine the extent of these private benefits. The results of studies of similar programs such as the Baltimore Options Program suggest that small earnings gains can be realized by welfare recipients even though the benefits may not outweigh the full costs funded by taxpayers.

7

Concluding Comments

The ET program in Massachusetts was introduced with high hopes in October of 1983. It has been declared a success by the Dukakis administration. However, these claims appear to be gross exaggerations.

The AFDC-Basic caseload did decline by 25 percent in Massachusetts over the 1978-83 period. But this decline occurred before ET was introduced and was primarily the result of the changes in the AFDC program brought about by the federal Omnibus Budget Reconciliation Act (OBRA) of 1981. During 1983-88, the AFDC caseload in Massachusetts declined by about three percent. However, this was a period of economic boom in Massachusetts as well as in much of the Northeast. And most of the states in the Northeast also experienced declines in their welfare caseloads that were as large or larger than those in Massachusetts. For example, over the 1983-88 period the New York and Rhode Island caseloads declined by about three percent, the Connecticut caseload by 12.5 percent, and the New Jersey caseload by 17 percent.

In this study, detailed statistical analyses were conducted of the determinants of the size of the Massachusetts AFDC caseload and of the welfare participation rate. After changes in economic conditions, welfare benefit levels, and the characteristics of single mothers were taken into account, ET was not found to be associated with any reduction in the AFDC caseload or in welfare participation rates. Massachusetts has remained a state where single mothers are more likely to participate in welfare than are similarly situated women in other states. Also, single mothers are less likely to work in Massachusetts than elsewhere, despite the implementation of ET.

Certain management aspects of the ET program may have worked against a more positive outcome. The program has emphasized as its primary goal, the production of a target number of job placements at relatively high wages. Initially DPW (*FY87 Budget Request,* January 1986) had a five-year plan to "place 50,000 recipients into jobs and save the taxpayers $150 million in welfare costs." To implement the plan, DPW adopted a system of performance-based contracting under which contractors are fully reimbursed only for placing participants in "priority jobs" (that is, jobs paying a rate at least equal to a designated floor) and only after the client has remained on the job for at least 30 days. Although this form of performance-based contracting may well spur the contractors to place more individuals in jobs, it also provides an incentive for them to try to attract those applicants who can most readily qualify for "priority jobs." As a result, contractors may fulfill the goal of placing a certain number of individuals in jobs at target wages. But these successful individuals are likely to be the more motivated and skilled participants who would have found jobs readily on their own.[1]

It is a common finding of evaluations of employment and training programs that program impacts are greater for those who are below average in terms of their employability, as evidenced by little prior work experience or longer term welfare dependence. Work programs seem to produce the largest behavioral changes for this group.[2] These less skilled participants, however, are not likely to contribute the most to job placement rates. Even after successful training, their earnings and

---

[1]   Data from the Urban Institute study show that more than 25 percent of ET job finders had one or more years of college training, which is exceptionally high compared to the average AFDC recipient.

[2]   See chapter 2 for details about the difference in program impacts between those with and without prior jobs skills.

employment rates are likely to lag behind those of participants with strong prior work skills. By basing their reimbursements to contractors on job placements at relatively high wage rates, the administrators of ET may have inadvertently provided an incentive for contractors to avoid those who seem harder to place, but who nevertheless have the most potential for experiencing true net gains. Moreover, this tendency is likely to be reinforced by the voluntary aspect of the program, since welfare recipients who are least motivated to work and most inclined towards long-term welfare dependence are probably least likely to volunteer.

One recommendation that emerges from this analysis is to refocus the program. The emphasis on numbers of job placements in "priority" jobs may produce an impressive announcement on the evening news, but it does not, as we have seen, produce real results in terms of reducing the welfare caseload. A more useful goal for ET contractors would be to help welfare recipients find better jobs more quickly than they could on their own. With limited resources, the program should provide the most help to recipients whose prospects for job success are the least favorable. This would mean modifying the system of performance-based contracting and eliminating the wage floor. More flexible methods for evaluating contractors should be developed that take into account the clientele served. Welfare recipients differ considerably in their skills, background and motivation, and there is no single numerical target that can be sensibly applied to everyone.

Consideration should also be given to making participation in ET mandatory and to varying the nature of the participation requirement depending on the person's background and skills. For example, recent AFDC entrants with prior work experience might be required to search for a job as are recipients of unemployment insurance. Long-term AFDC recipients might be required to participate in more intensive programs, perhaps on a continuing basis. Although we do not find that ET has been successful overall in reducing welfare participation, it is possible that some aspects of the program have been successful while others have not. In its final report, the Urban Institute will presumably provide data and analysis bearing on the effectiveness of different program treatments for different types of participants.

Another factor possibly limiting the effectiveness of ET is that certain program features may have actually attracted families onto AFDC in order to receive ET benefits. For example, some single mothers may have gone on welfare to obtain the more costly training for high-skill jobs, the extended Medicaid benefits or the generous child care assistance (which for two children can amount to a subsidy of more than $8,000 per year). If this turns out to be true, then the state may want to de-couple these benefits from the welfare program, making them available to the low-income working poor, whether or not they have been on welfare. Research is needed on the extent to which ET services may have been a factor in both case openings and case closings.

Research is also needed on the effects of alternative levels and types of child care expenditures on children's well-being and on the mother's employment. The Massachusetts program is costly because it favors formal day care programs subject to stringent requirements and regulations. Would less expensive modes such as family care be worth more per dollar spent? Is structured care particularly beneficial for children with special problems but not necessarily for the average child? These are questions that need to be addressed because half of the expenditures on ET at present fund child care services, although the effectiveness of these services is not known.

There is a larger issue to be considered, and that is the role of a work program in an overall policy to reduce welfare dependency and increase self-sufficiency. The relatively high benefit levels in Massachusetts (and other states in the Northeast) create disincentives for self-support and marriage particularly among lower income individuals. In some states this is reinforced by liberal eligibility policies, such as the Massachusetts policy to provide benefits to pregnant unmarried women without any children starting in the first month of their pregnancy. The burden of reversing the disincentive effects of welfare benefits is then placed on a work-related program which, it is hoped, will increase the potential earnings of welfare recipients enough to provide a new incentive to go off welfare. As the history of work programs shows, it has proven exceedingly difficult to devise programs that raise earnings enough to achieve this goal. Because of limited options, however, administrators of welfare programs have persisted in developing work programs for welfare recipients.

It is not likely that a work program alone can be the answer to welfare dependency. What is required is a change in attitudes that will prevent young women from viewing welfare as a long-term option for support. A mandatory requirement to participate in a work/training program might help in this regard. It may also be worthwhile to experiment with ways to reduce benefits after a period of time. With such a policy in place new AFDC recipients would have an additional incentive to take steps to become self-sufficient.

Broader programs of a preventive nature are to be encouraged. As is now widely recognized, elementary and secondary education need to be revamped so that young people, in particular those exposed to disadvantaged environments, can obtain the basic skills needed for successful lives. Improvements in schooling, which make labor market alternatives a reality, may help forestall the early childbearing that often leads to future welfare dependence.

Stricter collection of child support payments from absent fathers is another important measure to be taken. The record of payment by absent fathers, particularly when the mother is on welfare, is deplorably low nationwide, although Massachusetts is doing better in collection than most other states. Such efforts may have the added long-run benefit of encouraging more responsible behavior among couples concerning childbearing decisions.

Employment and training programs for welfare recipients have existed for many years. Evaluations of these programs have usually found that at best they have had modest impacts on earnings, employment, and welfare dependency. Against these prior findings, it should not come as a great surprise that ET has not reduced the AFDC caseload or increased the employment of single mothers in Massachusetts.

Our findings, however, raise a number of questions. Do the poor results for ET reflect particular design features unique to the program or do they reflect more basic limitations that any work-related program would encounter? Studies conducted by MDRC find that experimental work programs for AFDC recipients vary in their effects from state to state — some show positive outcomes while others have no effect at all. No rigorous analysis of the reasons for these differences appears to have been conducted. The approach that we have used relies on an aggregate analysis of an actual program over a long period of time. It does not delve into program detail as much as might be possible with a randomized experiment. However, randomized experiments may miss some of the effects that would be present if an experimental program were actually implemented on a large scale.

The kind of analysis we have done is much less costly than a randomized experiment and could be replicated in other states that have conducted work programs on a large scale. In view of the high hopes raised by the Family Support Act of 1988, which was partly modeled after ET, it is extremely important that more comparative analysis be conducted of the disparate results of the studies of existing state work programs for welfare recipients.

Appendix

Variable Definitions for Cross-Sectional Analysis
of CPS Samples of Single Mothers

Dichotomous variables (0, 1):

BLACK	Individual is black
OTHER	Individual is other non-White
HISPANIC	Individual is of Hispanic origin
SINGLE	Never married
WID-DIV	Widowed or divorced
DISABL	Disabled
SMSA	Lives in an SMSA
MASS	Lives in Massachusetts
AGELT25	Less than age 25
AGEGT40	Older than age 40
MIGRATE	Lived in a different state in preceding year
SOUTH	Lives in the southern region of the U.S.

Other variables:

SCHOOL	Years of school completed
CHI-18	Number of children under age 18
CHI-05	Number of children 5 years old or younger
STATE UN	Unemployment rate (percent) in the individual's state in the specific year
STATE INC	Per capita income (in thousands) in the individual's state in the specific year
AFDC BEN	AFDC maximum benefit for a family of four with no other income, in the individual's state in the given year (monthly benefit in hundreds)
CHI AID	Child support income from the absent father received during the year (in thousands)

Note:

The sample size for each year for Tables A-1 and A-2 is approximately 5,000 persons. The sample size for each year for Tables A-3 and A-4 is approximately 4,000 persons. Sample sizes for Tables A-5 and A-6 are given in the tables.

Source:

Public Use files of the Current Population Surveys, March Supplements.

Table A-1

Women Heading Primary Families or Sub-families (with own child present)

Dependent variable: Whether Received One Month or More of Public Assistance

Independent Variable	1980	1981	1982	1983	1984	1985	1986	1987
INTERCEP	0.4584	0.4674	0.4323	0.3713	0.5366	0.6521	0.5213	0.4152
	(6.14)	(5.91)	(5.56)	(4.84)	(7.26)	(8.63)	(6.82)	(5.21)
BLACK	0.0971	0.1102	0.1015	0.1327	0.1081	0.1087	0.0800	0.1083
	(6.15)	(6.74)	(6.32)	(8.30)	(6.93)	(6.96)	(5.14)	(6.97)
OTHER	0.0177	0.0120	0.0132	-0.0011	-0.0376	-0.0516	-0.0573	-0.0068
	(0.54)	(0.35)	(0.41)	(-0.03)	(-1.16)	(-1.56)	(-1.73)	(-0.21)
HISPANIC	0.0470	0.0327	0.0482	0.0455	0.0563	0.0775	0.0334	0.0475
	(2.51)	(1.71)	(2.52)	(2.43)	(3.03)	(4.30)	(1.82)	(2.64)
SINGLE	0.1663	0.1193	0.1051	0.1298	0.1076	0.1282	0.0896	0.1276
	(8.65)	(6.32)	(5.81)	(7.01)	(6.01)	(7.33)	(5.09)	(7.33)
WID-DIV	-0.0263	-0.5010	-0.0453	-0.0347	-0.0276	-0.0387	-0.0061	-0.0294
	(-1.86)	(-3.35)	(-2.99)	(-2.27)	(-1.82)	(-2.54)	(-0.39)	(-1.88)
SCHOOL	-0.0311	-0.0275	-0.0278	-0.0287	-0.0292	-0.0328	-0.0336	-0.0326
	(-13.26)	(-11.20)	(-11.33)	(-11.54)	(-12.12)	(-13.20)	(-13.40)	(-13.40)
DISABL	0.2403	0.2440	0.1485	0.2128	0.3389	0.2334	0.2703	0.1954
	(7.98)	(8.03)	(4.62)	(6.03)	(10.35)	(7.02)	(8.19)	(5.88)
MIGRATE	-0.0088	-0.0363	-0.0544	0.0021	0.0210	-0.0698	-0.0885	-0.0227
	(-0.31)	(-1.23)	(-1.81)	(0.07)	(1.18)	(-2.25)	(-2.72)	(-7.05)
CHI-18	0.0740	0.0664	0.0720	0.0726	0.0795	0.0863	0.0827	0.0815
	(11.78)	(10.0)	(10.90)	(10.40)	(11.73)	(12.60)	(12.10)	(11.90)
CHI-05	0.0749	0.0954	0.0807	0.0737	0.0779	0.0714	0.0718	0.0764
	(6.71)	(8.60)	(7.41)	(6.66)	(7.13)	(6.54)	(6.65)	(7.28)
AGELT25	0.1041	0.0515	0.0656	0.0693	0.0443	0.0361	0.0613	0.0163
	(5.23)	(2.63)	(3.41)	(3.62)	(2.35)	(1.90)	(3.24)	(0.86)
AGEGT40	-0.0878	-0.0634	-0.0327	-0.0303	-0.0367	-0.028	-0.0538	-0.0354
	(-5.90)	(-4.03)	(-2.04)	(-1.91)	(-2.35)	(-1.77)	(-3.35)	(-2.19)
STATE UN	0.0081	0.0047	0.0075	0.0107	0.0083	-0.0029	0.0041	0.0092
	(2.12)	(1.29)	(2.57)	(3.60)	(2.49)	(-0.76)	(1.17)	(2.48)
STATE INC	-0.0177	-0.0175	-0.0127	-0.0047	-0.0136	-0.0116	-0.0021	0.0034
	(-2.81)	(-2.90)	(-2.33)	(-0.94)	(-2.81)	(-2.66)	(-0.49)	(0.81)
AFDC BEN	0.0496	0.0511	0.0319	0.0197	0.0217	0.0188	0.0131	0.0069
	(6.43)	(6.62)	(4.03)	(2.65)	(3.14)	(2.88)	(2.08)	(1.12)
SOUTH	-0.0529	-0.0563	-0.0864	-0.1169	-0.1309	-0.1409	-0.1317	-0.1105
	(-2.69)	(-2.80)	(-4.23)	(-5.93)	(-7.10)	(-7.72)	(-7.39)	(-6.23)
SMSA	-0.0071	-0.0082	0.0275	-0.0023	-0.0140	-0.0133	-0.0137	-0.0520
	(-0.52)	(-0.60)	(2.01)	(-0.17)	(-1.04)	(-1.05)	(-1.06)	(-3.99)
MASS	0.1563	0.1036	0.1165	0.0289	0.0180	0.0837	0.1079	0.1009
	(4.02)	(2.52)	(2.71)	(0.69)	(0.52)	(2.59)	(3.36)	(3.21)
CHIAID	-0.0168	-0.0158	-0.0194	-0.0120	-0.0177	-0.0162	-0.018	-0.0082
	(-6.96)	(-6.93)	(-7.25)	(-5.40)	(-7.16)	(-7.48)	(-6.98)	(-4.32)
ADJ R-SQ	0.2468	0.2337	0.2189	0.2137	0.2270	0.2499	0.2134	0.2248

Table A-2

Women Heading Primary Families or Sub-families (with own child present)

Dependent Variable: Whether Worked During the Year

Independent Variable	1980	1981	1982	1983	1984	1985	1986	1987
INTERCEP	0.4743	0.5970	0.4888	0.6029	0.6043	0.4849	0.5301	0.5967
	(6.29)	(7.52)	(6.14)	(7.71)	(8.14)	(6.32)	(6.92)	(7.49)
BLACK	-0.0501	-0.0826	-0.0782	-0.1068	-0.0602	-0.0577	-0.0615	-0.0763
	(-3.15)	(-5.03)	(-4.77)	(-6.55)	(-3.84)	(-3.64)	(-3.95)	(-4.91)
OTHER	-0.0359	-0.0677	0.0104	-0.0587	-0.0710	-0.0893	-0.0414	-0.0855
	(-1.09)	(-1.97)	(0.32)	(-1.80)	(-2.18)	(-2.66)	(-1.25)	(-2.67)
HISPANIC	-0.0718	-0.0788	-0.0530	-0.0934	-0.0715	-0.0802	-0.0812	-0.0658
	(-3.80)	(-4.10)	(-2.71)	(-4.89)	(-3.83)	(-4.38)	(-4.42)	(-3.65)
SINGLE	-0.0580	-0.0777	-0.0794	-0.0553	-0.0759	-0.0715	-0.0607	-0.0557
	(-2.99)	(-4.10)	(-4.29)	(-2.93)	(-4.22)	(-4.02)	(-3.44)	(-3.20)
WID-DIV	0.0647	0.0594	0.0518	0.0494	0.0493	0.0503	0.0462	0.0607
	(4.55)	(3.96)	(3.34)	(3.16)	(3.24)	(3.24)	(2.98)	(3.89)
SCHOOL	0.0357	0.0348	0.0353	0.0343	0.0338	0.0390	0.0395	0.0388
	(15.06)	(14.10)	(14.06)	(13.51)	(13.98)	(15.40)	(15.80)	(15.90)
DISABL	-0.6466	-0.6271	-0.6082	-0.6133	-0.6579	-0.6126	-0.6268	-0.6086
	(-21.27)	(-20.5)	(-18.50)	(-17.03)	(-19.99)	(-18.1)	(-18.9)	(-18.3)
MIGRATE	-0.0242	-0.0027	-0.0446	-0.0321	-0.0407	0.0041	-0.0053	-0.0483
	(-0.84)	(-0.09)	(-1.52)	(-0.98)	(-2.27)	(0.13)	(-0.16)	(-1.50)
CHI-18	-0.0543	-0.0484	-0.0498	-0.0639	-0.0675	-0.0689	-0.0672	-0.0602
	(-8.57)	(-7.29)	(-7.38)	(-8.98)	(-9.91)	(-9.92)	(-9.80)	(-8.80)
CHI-05	-0.0921	-0.0941	-0.0896	-0.1114	-0.0986	-0.0928	-0.0795	-0.0856
	(-8.17)	(-8.45)	(-8.05)	(-9.88)	(-8.99)	(-8.37)	(-7.36)	(-8.15)
AGELT25	-0.0481	-0.0819	-0.1372	-0.1145	-0.0943	-0.0932	0.0877	-0.0726
	(-2.39)	(-4.17)	(-6.98)	(-5.87)	(-4.98)	(-4.82)	(-4.62)	(-3.85)
AGEGT40	-0.0276	-0.0249	-0.0258	-0.0210	-0.0514	-0.0052	0.0001	-0.0104
	(-1.84)	(-1.57)	(-1.58)	(-1.30)	(-3.27)	(-0.32)	(0.05)	(-0.65)
STATE UN	-0.0233	-0.02	-0.0121	-0.0120	-0.0157	-0.0077	-0.0117	-0.0142
	(-5.99)	(-5.50)	(-4.03)	(-3.95)	(-4.72)	(-2.01)	(-3.35)	(-3.84)
STATE INC	0.0219	0.0067	0.0039	-0.0026	-0.0003	-0.0015	-0.0065	-0.0078
	(3.45)	(1.11)	(0.70)	(-0.51)	(-0.06)	(-0.33)	(-1.50)	(-1.88)
AFDC BEN	-0.0302	-0.0265	-0.0069	-0.0076	-0.0048	-0.0088	-0.0023	-0.0035
	(-3.88)	(-3.41)	(-0.85)	(-1.00)	(-0.70)	(-1.32)	(-0.36)	(-0.57)
SOUTH	-0.0062	0.0022	0.0740	0.0645	0.0559	0.0547	0.0795	0.0423
	(-0.31)	(0.11)	(3.55)	(3.21)	(3.02)	(2.96)	(4.45)	(2.39)
SMSA	-0.0207	-0.0050	-0.0418	-0.0107	-0.0399	-0.0032	0.0046	-0.0116
	(-1.51)	(-0.37)	(-2.98)	(-0.77)	(-2.94)	(-0.25)	(0.36)	(-0.89)
MASS	-0.0337	-0.0878	-0.0443	0.0015	-0.0108	-0.0727	-0.0541	-0.0559
	(-0.86)	(-2.13)	(-1.01)	(0.04)	(-0.31)	(-2.22)	(-1.68)	(-1.78)
CHIAID	-0.0009	-0.0009	-0.0006	-0.0001	0.0057	0.0046	0.0011	-0.0008
	(-0.35)	(-0.40)	(-0.22)	(-0.05)	(2.29)	(2.08)	(0.43)	(-0.43)
ADJ R-SQ	0.2368	0.2470	0.2407	0.2390	0.2513	0.2571	0.2410	0.2509

Table A-3

Women Heading Primary Families (with own child present)

Dependent Variable: Whether Received One Month or More of Public Assistance

Independent Variable	1980	1981	1982	1983	1984	1985	1986	1987
INTERCEP	0.4595	0.5483	0.5050	0.3856	0.5154	0.6858	0.5352	0.5574
	(5.80)	(6.42)	(6.00)	(4.64)	(6.44)	(8.32)	(6.45)	(6.41)
BLACK	0.0891	0.0893	0.0982	0.1318	0.0976	0.0951	0.0691	0.1035
	(5.32)	(5.01)	(5.53)	(7.46)	(5.68)	(5.46)	(4.00)	(5.98)
OTHER	0.0590	0.0152	0.0056	0.0136	0.0073	-0.0027	-0.0652	0.0350
	(1.63)	(.392)	(.160)	(.379)	(.195)	(-.070)	(-1.70)	(.990)
HISPANIC	0.0538	0.0307	0.0519	0.0780	0.0658	0.0079	0.0345	0.0532
	(2.68)	(1.48)	(2.48)	(3.74)	(3.19)	(3.95)	(1.71)	(2.67)
SINGLE	0.1512	0.1385	0.1470	0.1542	0.1302	0.1480	0.1188	0.1551
	(7.27)	(6.46)	(7.10)	(7.24)	(6.44)	(7.52)	(6.03)	(7.92)
WID-DIV	-0.0402	-0.0759	-0.0478	-0.0365	-0.0360	-0.0494	-0.0180	-0.0334
	(-2.65)	(-4.80)	(-2.96)	(-2.25)	(-2.23)	(-3.03)	(-1.09)	(-2.00)
SCHOOL	-0.0314	-0.0295	-0.0321	-0.0292	-0.0323	-0.0371	-0.0350	-0.0364
	(-12.7)	(-11.4)	(-12.3)	(-10.9)	(-12.5)	(-13.9)	(-13.2)	(-13.9)
DISABL	0.2402	0.2542	0.2078	0.2203	0.3457	0.2408	0.3100	0.2350
	(7.54)	(7.76)	(5.84)	(5.68)	(9.75)	(6.70)	(8.49)	(6.58)
MIGRATE	0.0188	0.0050	0.0339	0.0016	0.0261	-0.0410	-0.0606	-0.0462
	(.570)	(.139)	(.910)	(.043)	(1.31)	(-1.15)	(-1.52)	(-1.19)
CHI-18	0.0741	0.0557	0.0626	0.0660	0.0721	0.0792	0.0780	0.0725
	(11.3)	(8.14)	(9.03)	(9.04)	(10.1)	(10.9)	(10.9)	(9.89)
CHI-05	0.0866	0.1022	0.0871	0.0882	0.0811	0.0688	0.0700	0.0835
	(7.18)	(8.50)	(7.24)	(7.26)	(6.70)	(5.74)	(5.84)	(7.15)
AGELT25	0.1595	0.1296	0.1610	0.1598	0.1446	0.1057	0.1600	0.0925
	(6.92)	(5.36)	(6.66)	(6.60)	(6.11)	(4.42)	(6.70)	(3.90)
AGEGT40	-0.0819	-0.0747	-0.0467	-0.0273	-0.0437	-0.0366	-0.0572	-0.0466
	(-5.35)	(-4.66)	(-2.87)	(-1.69)	(-2.73)	(-2.24)	(-3.47)	(-2.80)
STATE UN	0.0065	0.0031	0.0074	0.0114	0.0107	-0.0014	0.0046	0.0041
	(1.60)	(.794)	(2.33)	(3.54)	(2.95)	(-.344)	(1.20)	(.998)
STATE INC	-0.0152	-0.0143	-0.0116	-0.0056	-0.0084	-0.0062	-0.0004	0.0002
	(-2.28)	(-2.20)	(-1.95)	(-1.00)	(-1.59)	(-1.29)	(-.077)	(.052)
AFDC BEN	0.0477	0.0441	0.0304	0.0189	0.0207	0.0115	0.0108	0.0079
	(5.78)	(5.25)	(3.52)	(2.31)	(2.73)	(1.59)	(1.57)	(1.16)
SOUTH	-0.0468	-0.0727	-0.0965	-0.1273	-0.1349	-0.1476	-0.1273	-0.1061
	(-2.23)	(-3.30)	(-4.33)	(-5.86)	(-6.63)	(-7.33)	(-6.49)	(-5.45)
SMSA	-0.0003	0.0019	0.0329	0.0130	-0.0094	-0.0119	-0.0058	-0.0416
	(-.019)	(.129)	(2.20)	(.878)	(-.640)	(-.856)	(-.404)	(-2.89)
MASS	0.1623	0.0865	0.0765	0.0250	0.0215	0.0737	0.0980	0.1008
	(4.11)	(2.01)	(1.66)	(.562)	(.580)	(2.12)	(2.87)	(3.03)
CHIAID	-0.0172	-0.0161	-0.0181	-0.0109	-0.0170	-0.0160	-0.0176	-0.0077
	(-7.09)	(-7.07)	(-6.82)	(-5.01)	(-6.89)	(-7.37)	(-6.83)	(-4.07)
ADJ R-SQ	0.2788	0.2817	0.2833	0.2625	0.2844	0.2974	0.2651	0.2787

Table A-4

Women Heading Primary Families (with own child present)

Dependent Variable: Whether Worked During the Year

Independent Variable	1980	1981	1982	1983	1984	1985	1986	1987
INTERCEP	0.5420	0.6874	0.4731	0.6099	0.6632	0.5037	0.5805	0.6185
	(6.77)	(8.03)	(5.45)	(7.19)	(8.25)	(6.05)	(6.97)	(7.16)
BLACK	-0.0492	-0.0648	-0.0639	-0.0899	-0.0558	-0.0506	-0.0583	-0.0725
	(-2.90)	(-3.63)	(-3.49)	(-4.98)	(-3.23)	(-2.87)	(-3.36)	(-4.22)
OTHER	-0.0513	-0.0569	0.0162	-0.0393	-0.0757	-0.0555	0.0090	-0.0918
	(-1.40)	(-1.46)	(.446)	(-1.07)	(-2.00)	(-1.43)	(.235)	(-2.61)
HISPANIC	-0.0868	-0.0751	-0.0428	-0.1077	-0.0805	-0.0983	-0.0830	-0.0928
	(-4.28)	(-3.62)	(-1.98)	(-5.07)	(-3.88)	(-4.87)	(-4.09)	(-4.68)
SINGLE	-0.0620	-0.0847	-0.0815	-0.0668	-0.0678	-0.0892	-0.0536	-0.0772
	(-2.95)	(-3.94)	(-3.82)	(-3.07)	(-3.33)	(-4.49)	(-2.71)	(-3.97)
WID-DIV	0.0671	0.0573	0.0437	0.0448	0.0406	0.0448	0.0508	0.0543
	(4.39)	(3.61)	(2.62)	(2.70)	(2.50)	(2.71)	(3.07)	(3.27)
SCHOOL	0.0352	0.0337	0.0381	0.0335	0.0351	0.0394	0.0383	0.0367
	(14.1)	(12.9)	(14.2)	(12.2)	(13.5)	(14.6)	(14.4)	(14.1)
DISABL	-0.6489	-0.6325	-0.6318	-0.6421	-0.6664	-0.6020	-0.6448	-0.6322
	(-20.2)	(-19.2)	(-17.2)	(-16.2)	(-18.7)	(-16.6)	(-17.6)	(-17.8)
MIGRATE	-0.0293	0.0232	-0.0286	-0.0368	-0.0494	-0.0240	0.0154	-0.0338
	(-.878)	(.649)	(-.744)	(-.951)	(-2.48)	(-.668)	(.384)	(-.879)
CHI-18	-0.0583	-0.0570	-0.0559	-0.0698	-0.0670	-0.0687	-0.0714	-0.0660
	(-8.82)	(-8.30)	(-7.82)	(-9.36)	(-9.35)	(-9.33)	(-9.93)	(-9.08)
CHI-05	-0.0946	-0.1055	0.0940	-0.1158	-0.1045	-0.0888	-0.0732	-0.0866
	(-7.76)	(-8.76)	(-7.58)	(-9.33)	(-8.59)	(-7.32)	(-6.10)	(-7.47)
AGELT25	-0.0541	-0.0493	-0.1167	-0.1094	-0.0843	-0.0919	-0.0933	-0.0452
	(-2.32)	(-2.03)	(-4.68)	(-4.42)	(-3.54)	(-3.80)	(-3.89)	(-1.92)
AGEGT40	-0.0420	-0.0410	-0.0226	-0.0346	-0.0534	-0.0060	-0.0074	-0.0173
	(-2.71)	(-2.55)	(-1.35)	(-2.10)	(-3.31)	(-.365)	(-.447)	(-1.04)
STATE UN	-0.0249	-0.0197	-0.0117	-0.0122	-0.0180	-0.0079	-0.0111	-0.0099
	(-6.04)	(-4.98)	(-3.56)	(-3.73)	(-4.93)	(-1.87)	(-2.86)	(-2.45)
STATE INC	0.0168	0.0027	0.0034	-0.0011	-0.0065	-0.0022	-0.0071	-0.0077
	(2.50)	(.418)	(.551)	(-.187)	(-1.22)	(-.462)	(-1.51)	(-1.69)
AFDC BEN	-0.0259	-0.0279	-0.0071	-0.0033	0.0022	-0.0107	-0.0064	-0.0040
	(-3.10)	(-3.31)	(-.797)	(-.395)	(.292)	(-1.47)	(-.931)	(-.587)
SOUTH	-0.0006	0.0066	0.0791	0.0872	0.0773	0.0578	0.0657	0.0327
	(-.026)	(.300)	(3.44)	(3.93)	(3.78)	(2.84)	(3.34)	(1.69)
SMSA	-0.0202	-0.0088	-0.0458	-0.0268	-0.0411	0.0051	0.0031	0.0012
	(-1.38)	(-.597)	(-2.97)	(-1.78)	(-2.78)	(.361)	(.215)	(.081)
MASS	-0.0444	-0.0873	-0.0411	-0.0269	-0.0163	-0.0801	-0.0678	-0.0570
	(-1.11)	(-2.03)	(-.864)	(-.593)	(-.438)	(-2.28)	(-1.98)	(-1.72)
CHIAID	-0.0012	-0.0003	-0.0007	-0.0012	0.0046	0.0041	0.0011	-0.0005
	(-.489)	(-.146)	(-.246)	(-.519)	(1.86)	(1.85)	(.440)	(-.243)
ADJ R-SQ	0.2528	0.2634	0.2532	0.2551	0.2748	0.2810	0.2546	0.2747

Table A-5

White Non-Hispanic Women Heading Primary Families or Sub-families (with own child present)

Dependent Variable: Whether Received One Month or More of Public Assistance

Independent Variable	1980	1981	1982	1983	1984	1985	1986	1987
INTERCEP	0.4807	0.6051	0.4154	0.4634	0.5510	0.6913	0.5521	0.5778
	(5.00)	(5.88)	(4.00)	(4.71)	(5.46)	(7.11)	(5.46)	(5.48)
SINGLE	0.2025	0.1824	0.1628	0.2441	0.1515	0.1683	0.2133	0.2058
	(6.11)	(5.19)	(4.82)	(7.19)	(4.44)	(5.52)	(6.90)	(6.73)
WID-DIV	-0.0003	-0.0285	-0.0118	0.0180	0.0079	-0.0032	0.0504	-0.0116
	(-.014)	(-1.45)	(-.566)	(.887)	(.364)	(-.157)	(2.40)	(-.549)
SCHOOL	-0.0337	-0.0363	-0.0356	-0.0364	-0.0372	-0.0379	-0.0369	-0.0368
	(-9.63)	(-9.97)	(-9.98)	(-9.83)	(-9.92)	(-10.3)	(-9.92)	(-9.81)
DISABL	0.2643	0.2690	0.1746	0.3964	0.3623	0.2095	0.3858	0.2946
	(5.96)	(5.39)	(3.07)	(6.64)	(7.05)	(3.85)	(7.66)	(5.64)
CHI-18	0.0638	0.0348	0.0646	0.0564	0.0562	0.0614	0.0715	0.0821
	(6.72)	(3.64)	(6.47)	(5.66)	(5.16)	(5.89)	(6.81)	(7.67)
CHI-05	0.1114	0.1156	0.0883	0.0851	0.1065	0.1014	0.0809	0.0845
	(6.56)	(6.96)	(5.30)	(5.30)	(6.12)	(6.15)	(4.80)	(5.21)
AGELT25	0.1486	0.1271	0.1241	0.1004	0.2052	0.0849	0.1523	0.0455
	(4.80)	(3.95)	(3.79)	(3.14)	(6.10)	(2.73)	(4.75)	(1.39)
AGEGT40	-0.0911	-0.0852	-0.0332	-0.0341	-0.0346	-0.0426	-0.0461	-0.0250
	(-4.95)	(-4.45)	(-1.68)	(-1.78)	(-1.76)	(-2.20)	(-2.31)	(-1.23)
STATE UN	0.0018	0.0027	0.0133	0.0089	0.0093	-0.0002	0.0066	0.0117
	(.389)	(.609)	(3.70)	(2.53)	(2.15)	(-.041)	(1.40)	(2.36)
STATE INC	-0.0180	-0.0144	-0.0153	-0.0107	-0.0120	-0.0150	-0.0096	-0.0082
	(-2.31)	(-1.86)	(-2.13)	(-1.66)	(-1.82)	(-2.64)	(1.67)	(-1.51)
AFDC BEN	0.0573	0.0511	0.0502	0.0347	0.0324	0.0300	0.0247	0.0121
	(5.74)	(4.99)	(4.63)	(3.51)	(3.31)	(3.37)	(2.86)	(1.42)
SOUTH	-0.0016	-0.0528	-0.0367	-0.0648	-0.0473	-0.0652	-0.0822	-0.0562
	(-.061)	(-1.99)	(-1.34)	(-2.48)	(-1.80)	(-2.67)	(-3.32)	(-2.31)
SMSA	0.0001	-0.0027	0.0276	-0.0072	-0.0251	-0.0226	-0.022	-0.0647
	(.006)	(-.151)	(1.48)	(-0.40)	(-1.31)	(-1.37)	(-1.28)	(-3.71)
MASS	0.1503	0.0478	0.0564	0.0278	-0.0158	0.0985	0.0488	0.1192
	(3.48)	(1.00)	(1.04)	(.554)	(-0.37)	(2.50)	(1.22)	(2.30)
CHIAID	-0.0134	0.0128	-0.0149	-0.0075	-0.0137	-0.0128	-0.0140	0.0059
	(-5.67)	(-5.70)	(-5.66)	(-3.55)	(-5.09)	(-5.93)	(-5.34)	(-3.23)
ADJ R-SQ	0.2479	0.2467	0.2247	0.2174	0.2573	0.2342	0.2376	0.2219
Sample size	2,324	2,159	2,057	2,073	1,925	2,076	2,141	2,064

Table A-6

White Non-Hispanic Women Heading Primary Families or
Sub-families (with own child present)

Dependent Variable: Whether Worked During the Year

Independent

Variable	1980	1981	1982	1983	1984	1985	1986	1987
INTERCEP	0.5537	0.5785	0.5109	0.5946	0.6470	0.4705	0.5790	0.6307
	(5.58)	(5.60)	(4.62)	(5.70)	(6.29)	(4.71)	(5.68)	(6.06)
SINGLE	-0.0646	-0.0548	-0.0817	-0.0589	-0.0658	-0.0944	-0.1015	-0.0668
	(-1.89)	(-1.55)	(-2.27)	(-1.63)	(-1.89)	(-3.01)	(-3.26)	(-2.21)
WID-DIV	0.0576	0.0628	0.0377	0.0283	0.0302	0.0195	0.0213	0.0464
	(2.91)	(3.17)	(1.70)	(1.31)	(1.37)	(.921)	(1.01)	(2.22)
SCHOOL	0.0345	0.0389	0.0441	0.0391	0.0345	0.0373	0.0359	0.0336
	(9.55)	(10.6)	(11.6)	(9.93)	(9.01)	(9.91)	(9.56)	(9.08)
DISABL	-0.7261	-0.7244	-0.6912	-0.7452	-0.7405	-0.7154	-0.7604	-0.7651
	(-15.9)	(-14.4)	(-11.4)	(-11.8)	(-14.13)	(-12.8)	(-15.0)	(-14.8)
CHI-18	-0.0537	-0.0439	-0.0547	-0.0698	-0.0591	-0.0524	-0.0830	-0.0649
	(-5.48)	(-4.56)	(-5.14)	(-6.60)	(-5.32)	(-4.89)	(-7.85)	(-6.14)
CHI-05	-0.1065	-0.1317	-0.0847	-0.1202	-0.1254	-0.1115	-0.0640	-0.0791
	(-6.07)	(-7.89)	(-4.77)	(-7.06)	(-7.07)	(-6.58)	(-3.76)	(-4.93)
AGELT25	0.0051	0.0313	-0.0666	-0.0699	-0.1281	-0.0808	-0.0987	-0.0069
	(.158)	(.968)	(-1.91)	(-2.06)	(-3.74)	(-2.52)	(-3.05)	(-.214)
AGEGT40	-0.0449	-0.0475	-0.0184	-0.0569	-0.0616	-0.0200	-0.0184	-0.0091
	(-2.36)	(-2.47)	(-.872)	(-2.80)	(-3.07)	(-1.01)	(-0.91)	(-.454)
STATE UN	-0.0178	-0.0196	-0.0154	-0.0102	-0.0131	-0.0083	-0.0130	-0.0103
	(3.70)	(-4.38)	(-4.02)	(-2.72)	(-2.97)	(-1.67)	(-2.71)	(-2.11)
STATE INC	0.0133	0.0059	-0.0010	-0.0045	-0.0057	0.0045	-0.0002	-0.0038
	(1.65)	(.759)	(-.126)	(-.665)	(-.851)	(.762)	(-.037)	(-.697)
AFDC BEN	-0.0293	-0.0326	-0.0138	-0.0064	-0.0025	-0.0174	-0.0073	-0.0108
	(-2.84)	(-3.17)	(-1.20)	(-.605)	(-.248)	(-1.89)	(-.834)	(-1.28)
SOUTH	-0.0383	-0.0443	0.0188	0.0407	0.0336	0.0213	0.0323	-0.0228
	(-1.43)	(-1.67)	(.644)	(1.47)	(-1.25)	(0.85)	(1.29)	(-.946)
SMSA	-0.0215	0.0202	-0.0336	-0.0125	-0.0049	0.0325	0.0262	0.0411
	(-1.17)	(1.12)	(-1.70)	(-.652)	(-.253)	(1.92)	(1.50)	(2.38)
MASS	-0.0469	-0.0308	-0.0465	-0.0319	0.0122	-0.0888	-0.0247	-0.0541
	(-1.05)	(-.641)	(-.806)	(-.599)	(0.280)	(-2.19)	(-.612)	(-.138)
CHIAID	-0.0004	-0.0018	-0.0029	-0.0022	0.0043	0.0041	-0.0003	0.0008
	(-.161)	(-.775)	(-1.05)	(-.981)	(1.58)	(1.83)	(-.114)	(-.470)
ADJ R-SQ	0.2030	0.2181	0.1951	0.1904	0.2376	0.2220	0.2109	0.2032
Sample size	2,324	2,159	2,057	2,073	1,925	2,076	2,141	2,064

Bibliography

Armstrong, David. "Study Rates ET Program a Success." *The Boston Herald,* November 28, 1989.

Bane, M. and D. Ellwood. *The Dynamics of Dependence: The Routes to Self-Sufficiency.* Cambridge, MA: Urban Systems Research and Engineering, Inc., 1983.

Barnow, Burt S. "Estimating the New Jersey AFDC Caseload." Washington, D.C.: U.S. Department of Health and Human Services, Office of the Assistant Secretary for Planning and Evaluation, February 1988.

Behn, Robert. *Managing Innovation in Welfare Training, and Work: Some lessons from ET Choices in Massachusetts.* Paper presented at the 1987 Annual Meeting of the American Political Science Association, Chicago, Illinois, September 4, 1987.

Brookes, Warren. "The Stunning Failure of Dukakis's ET." *The Wall Street Journal,* January 19, 1987.

Congressional Budget Office. *Work and Welfare: The Family Support Act of 1988.* January 1989.

Council of Economic Advisers. *Economic Report of the President.* Washington, D.C.: Government Printing Office, 1976.

Dukakis, Michael S. and Rosabeth Moss Kanter. *Creating the Future.* New York: Summit Books, 1988.

Ellwood, David T. "Targeting Would-Be Long-Term Recipients of AFDC." Washington, D.C.: U.S. Department of Health and Human Services, Office of the Assistant Secretary for Planning and Evaluation, January 1986.

Executive Office of the President, Interagency Low Income Opportunity Advisory Board. *Up From Dependency: A New National*

Public Assistance Strategy, Supplement 4: Research Studies and Bibliography. April 1988.

Freedman, Stephen, Jan Bryant, and George Cave. *New Jersey: Final Report on the Grant Diversion Project.* New York: Manpower Demonstration Research Corporation, November 1988.

Friedlander, Daniel. *Supplemental Report on the Baltimore Options Program.* New York: Manpower Demonstration Research Corporation, October 1987.

Friedlander, Daniel, Gregory Hoerz, Janet Quint, and James Riccio, with Barbara Goldman, Judith Gueron, and David Long. *Arkansas: Final Report on the WORK Program in Two Counties.* New York: Manpower Demonstration Research Corporation, 1985.

Friedlander, Daniel, Gregory Hoerz, David Long, and Janet Quint. *Maryland: Final Report on the Employment Initiatives Evaluation.* New York: Manpower Demonstration Research Corporation, December 1985.

Garasky, Steve. "Analyzing the Effect of Massachusetts' ET Choices Program on the State's AFDC Caseload." Washington, D.C.: U.S. Department of Health and Human Services, Office of the Assistant Secretary for Planning and Evaluation, June 1989.

Goldman, B., D. Friedlander and D. Long. *Final Report on the San Diego Job Search and Work Experience Demonstration.* New York: Manpower Demonstration Research Corporation, February 1986.

Grossman, J., R. Maynard and J. Roberts. "Reanalysis of the Effects of Selected Employment and Training Programs for Welfare Recipients." Princeton: Mathematica Policy Research, 1985.

Gueron, Judith M. *Work Initiatives For Welfare Recipients: Lessons from a Multi-State Experiment.* New York: Manpower Demonstration Research Corporation, March 1986.

Gueron, Judith M. "Work and Welfare: Lessons on Employment Programs," *Journal of Economic Perspectives,* Vol. 4, No. 1 (Winter 1990): 79-98.

Heckman, James J., V. Joseph Hotz, and Marcelo Dabos. "Do We Need Experimental Data to Evaluate the Impact of Manpower Training on Earnings?" *Evaluation Review* 11 (August 1987): 395-427.

Ketron, Inc. *The Long-Term Impact of WIN II: A Longitudinal Evaluation of the Employment Experiences of Participants in the Work Incentive Program.* Pennsylvania: Ketron, Inc., 1980.

Kindleberger, Richard. "Hub hit on job placement rate." *The Boston Globe,* July 27, 1989.

Kluver, Jean. "ET: Workfare Under Another Name, Or A Stepping Stone to Self Sufficiency?" Boston: American Friends Service Committee, March 1985.

Lalonde, Robert and Rebecca Maynard. "How Precise Are Evaluations of Employment and Training Programs: Evidence from a Field Experiment," *Evaluation Review* 11 (August 1987): 428-51.

Levitan, Sar A., Martin Rein and David Marwick. *Work and Welfare Go Together.* Baltimore: John Hopkins University Press, 1972.

Levy, Frank. "The Labor Supply of Female Heads, or AFDC Work Incentives Don't Work Too Well." *Journal of Human Resources* 14 (Winter 1979).

Lynch, John A., and Dave M. O'Neill. *Poverty and Public Policy.* Washington, D.C.: American Enterprise Institute, 1973.

Massachusetts Department of Public Welfare. *1979-1982 Budget.*

Massachusetts Department of Public Welfare. *FY 85 Budget Request.* June 13, 1984.

Massachusetts Department of Public Welfare. *Your right to know.*

Massachusetts Department of Public Welfare, Office of Research, Planning and Evaluation. *An Evaluation of the Massachusetts Employment and Training Choices Program: Interim Findings On Participation and Outcomes FY84-FY85.* January 1986.

Massachusetts Department of Public Welfare. *FY 87 Budget Request, Executive Summary.* January 22, 1986.

Massachusetts Department of Public Welfare. *An Analysis of the First 25,000 ET Placements.* August 1986.

Massachusetts Department of Public Welfare. *Removing Barriers to Opportunity: The Welfare Department's FY88 Budget Request.* February 13, 1987.

Massachusetts Department of Public Welfare. *FY89 Budget Narrative.*

Massachusetts Department of Public Welfare. *My Mom and ET.* September 1989.

Mass Home Care. *At Home with Mass Home Care.* Newsletter, September 1988.

Massachusetts Senate Committee on Ways and Means, *Policy Reports: Agenda '90, FY 1988 Budget, Volume Two.*

Massachusetts Taxpayers Foundation. *Training People to Live without Welfare.* Boston, 1987.

Mathematica Policy Research Incorporated. "Technical Report for the AFDC Forecasting Project." Washington, D.C.: U.S. Department of Health and Human Services, Social Security Administration, Office of Family Assistance, February 1985.

Moffitt, Robert. "Work and the U.S. Welfare System: A Review." Institute for Research on Poverty Special Report no. 46. April 1988.

Nightingale, Demetra Smith, L. C. Burbridge, D. Wissoker, L. Bawden, F. L. Sonenstein, and N. Jeffries. "Experiences of Massachusetts ET Job Finders: Preliminary Findings." Washington, D.C.: Urban Institute, October 1989.

O'Neill, J., L. Bassi and D. Wolf. "The Duration of Welfare Spells." *Review of Economic and Statistics* 69 (May 1987): 241-248.

O'Neill, J., D. Wolf, L. Bassi and M. T. Hannan. *An Analysis of Time on Welfare.* Final Report to the Department of Health and Human Services, Contract HHS-100-83-0048. June 1984.

Plotnick, Robert D., and Russell M. Lidman. "Forecasting Welfare Caseloads: A Tool to Improve Budgeting." *Public Budgeting & Finance.* Autumn 1987.

Ross, Heather L. and Isabel V. Sawhill. *Time of Transition.* Washington, D.C.: The Urban Institute, 1975.

Stein, Charles. "Massachusetts, N.H. differ in approach to poor." *The Boston Globe*, June 25, 1988.

Stein, Charles. "Progress in cutting roles is at standstill." *The Boston Globe*, June 23, 1988.

U. S. Bureau of the Census. *Current Population Surveys.* March Supplements, Public Use Files.

U. S. Bureau of the Census. *Estimates of Poverty Including the Value of Noncash Benefits: 1987.* Washington, D.C.

U. S. Department of Health and Human Services Family Support Administration, Office of Family Assistance. *Characteristics and Financial Circumstances of AFDC Recipients.* 1983 and 1987.

U. S. Department of Labor. " WIN for a Change." Washington, D.C., 1971.

U. S. House of Representatives, Committee on Ways and Means. *Background Material and Data on Programs within the Jurisdiction of the Committee of Ways and Means,* 1989 Edition.

U. S. General Accounting Office. *Work And Welfare, Analysis of AFDC Programs in Four States, GAO/HRD-88-33 FS.* January 1988.

About the Author

June O'Neill is the director of the Center for the Study of Business and Government and a professor in the department of economics at Baruch College, City University of New York. A leading social policy analyst, she has served as Director of the Office of Programs, Policy and Research at the U.S. Commission on Civil Rights, and as a Program Director and Senior Research Associate at the Urban Institute. Prior to that, she held senior research positions with the Congressional Budget Office, the President's Council of Economic Advisors and the Brookings Institution.

She has been widely published in scholarly journals and in public policy literature and has testified before congressional committees on many subjects, including poverty, welfare and social security, women's economic status, income differences among races, productivity in education, and tax policy.

Dr. O'Neill received her Bachelor's degree from Sarah Lawrence College and her PhD in Economics from Columbia University.

Pioneer Publications

In Print:

Pioneer Paper No. 1, *The Massachusetts Health Plan: The Right Prescription?* by Attiat F. Ott and Wayne B. Gray, Clark University, published 1988.

Pioneer Paper No. 2, *The Cost of Regulated Pricing: A Critical Analysis of Auto Insurance Premium Rate-Setting in Massachusetts,* by Simon Rottenberg, University of Massachusetts at Amherst, published 1989.

Pioneer Dialogue No. 1, *Thoughts on School Reform,* the proceedings of a Pioneer luncheon forum and two symposiums held at Harvard University, published 1989.

Pioneer Dialogue No. 2, *Bay State Auto Rates: What Are the Driving Forces?,* the proceedings of a Pioneer luncheon forum, published 1990.

Forthcoming:

Edward Moscovitch, economist, on Massachusetts mental retardation programs

Jeffrey Sedgwick, University of Massachusetts at Amherst and Kenneth Holland, University of Vermont, on legislative reform issues

Abigail Thernstrom, independent scholar, on school choice in Massachusetts